Set design by Rachel Hauck

Photo by Russell Caldwell

A scene from the La Jolla Playhouse production of *Be Aggressive*.

BE AGGRESSIVE
BY ANNIE WEISMAN

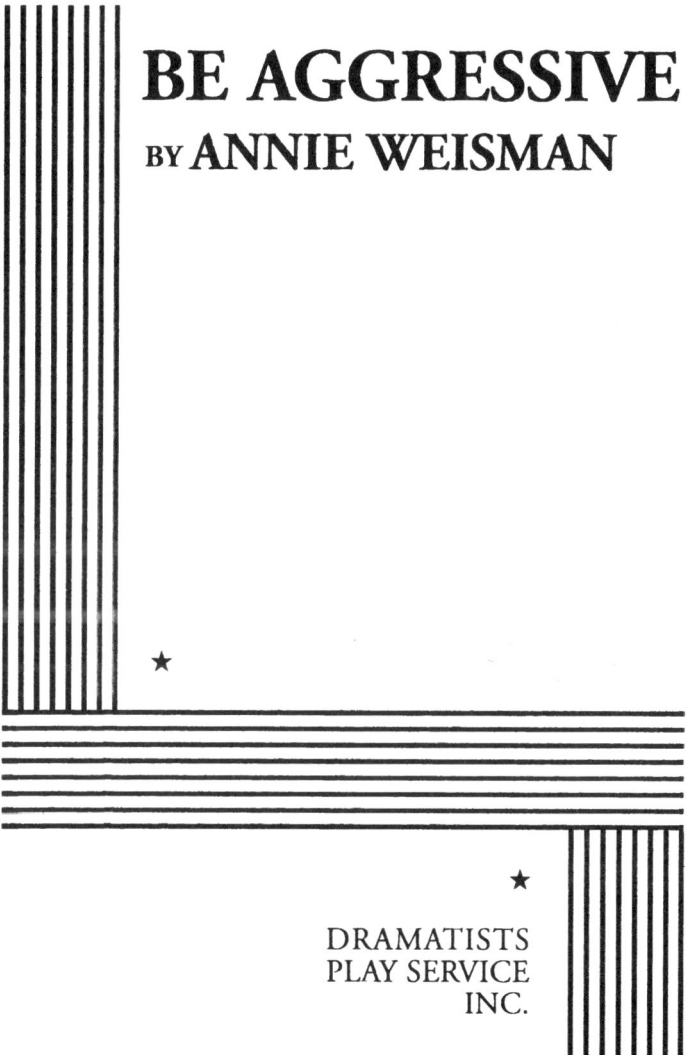

★

★

DRAMATISTS
PLAY SERVICE
INC.

for my sister

what would the music
be without you
since even through
the chorus of pure joy
the tears hear you
and nothing can restrain them.

—*from "To the Sorrow String"*
W.S. Merwin

BE AGGRESSIVE received its world premiere at the La Jolla Playhouse in La Jolla, California, on July 29, 2001. It was directed by Lisa Peterson; the set design was by Rachel Hauck; the lighting design was by James F. Ingalls; the sound design was by Laura Grace Brown; and the costume design was by Audrey Fisher. The cast in order of appearance was as follows:

LAURA .... Angela Goethals
HANNAH .... Daisy Eagan
PHIL .... Mark Harelik
LESLIE .... Jennifer Elise Cox
JUDY .... Linda Gehringer
CHEERLEADER CHORUS .... Tamala Horbianski
Carly Kleiner
Joy Osmanski

CHARACTERS
(in order of appearance)

LAURA, a 17-year-old girl

HANNAH, an 11-year-old girl

PHIL, a man in his mid-forties

LESLIE, a 17-year-old girl

JUDY, a woman in her mid-forties

PLACE

Vista Del Sol, a community by the sea in Southern California, and on the road. The play shifts quickly from scene to scene, and set design should be minimal. Sound, light, and only the most essential props and furniture should be used to suggest the various settings.

TIME

The present.

A Note on Casting: The author's intention is for adult actors to play Laura, Leslie and Hannah. The age plausibility should be theatrical, not literal.

7

BE AGGRESSIVE

ACT ONE

Prologue

In darkness, we hear the sound of the ocean, then the sound of the freeway, then the sound of a horrible car crash. Silence. Lights up. Bright sunshine. Vista Del Sol High-School-by-the-sea. Cheerleaders in formation. The sound of pom-poms shaking. The voices are choral and a little spooky.

CHEERLEADER #1. Did you guys hear?
CHEERLEADERS #3 and #4. Dead.
CHEERLEADER #2. Who?
CHEERLEADER #1. Dead.
CHEERLEADER #2. Who?
CHEERLEADERS #1, #3, and #4. Dead! *(Beat.)*
CHEERLEADER #3. Our maid's their maid's daughter.
CHEERLEADER #4. Our lawyer's their lawyer's son! *(Beat.)*
CHEERLEADER #3. My dermatologist lives on her cul-de-sac!
CHEERLEADER #4. My gynecologist lives next door!
CHEERLEADER #1. Dead. On impact.
CHEERLEADER #3. Nuh uh! Vegetable. All night.
CHEERLEADER #2. Fifteen feet it threw her.
CHEERLEADER #3. Fifty feet, I heard.
CHEERLEADER #1. The hole in her head was the size of a golf ball.
CHEERLEADER #2. Bocce ball!
CHEERLEADER #3. Honeydew!
CHEERLEADER #4. Canteloupe!

CHEERLEADER #1. It was on Avenida Avocado.

CHEERLEADER #2. That's where my stepmom power walks!

CHEERLEADER #1. They said that her dad had to come identify her mom's mangled body. *(They gasp. Beat.)* It's gonna be open casket.

CHEERLEADER #3. NUH UH!

CHEERLEADER #2. YEAH RIGHT!

CHEERLEADER #1. They're gonna have an open casket!

CHEERLEADER #3. NO WAY!

CHEERLEADER #2. YOU LIE!

CHEERLEADER #4. Pieces of her body are strewn across the street. *(All look out. Pause.)*

CHEERLEADER #1. I heard it's at the Surfswell Plaza Freeway Project.

CHEERLEADER #3. I heard she got so crushed that they're gonna pave part of her right into the new road.

CHEERLEADER #4. I heard that too.

CHEERLEADER #3. I heard her head hit like a hackey sack on a handball court.

CHEERLEADER #2. Like boobs on a boogie board.

CHEERLEADER #4. Splat!

CHEERLEADER #1. They drove away.

CHEERLEADER #2. Who?

CHEERLEADER #3. The ones who killed her.

CHEERLEADER #4. They hit her into a hole and they drove away. *(Beat.)* Vista Del Sol is like, a dangerous place. *(Pause. A light shift. A sudden change in mood.)*

CHEERLEADER #1. 'K guys! Practice!

CHEERLEADER #2. Without her?

CHEERLEADER #1. Without her.

CHEERLEADER #4. Is she coming back?

CHEERLEADER #2. Yeah, can she cheer any more?

CHEERLEADER #3. How long's it gonna take? We already made up our game-one greeting cheer! It's gonna be totally truncated without her!

CHEERLEADER #1. She'll be back. *(Beat.)* HANDS ON HIPS!

ALL. SMILES ON LIPS!

CHEERLEADER #1. *(A cheer.)* READY?

ALL. OK!
CHEERLEADER #1. H! *(CLAP!CLAP! CLAP!CLAP!)*
CHEERLEADER #2. E! *(CLAP!CLAP! CLAP!CLAP!)*
CHEERLEADER #3. L! *(CLAP!)*
CHEERLEADER #4. L! *(CLAP! They wait for the "O." It doesn't come. They continue.)*
CHEERLEADER #1. H! *(CLAP!CLAP! CLAP!CLAP!)*
CHEERLEADER #2. E! *(CLAP!CLAP! CLAP!CLAP!)*
CHEERLEADER #3. L! *(CLAP!)*
CHEERLEADER #4. L! *(CLAP! Clapping, stomping. Lights shift.)*

Scene 1

Lights up on Laura in her room with her little sister Hannah. They are getting dressed.

LAURA. O.
HANNAH. What?
LAURA. Nothing. *(Pause.)*
HANNAH. It's not fair.
LAURA. I know.
HANNAH. I don't have a whole black outfit. And you do. I only have separates. My blacks don't even match. It's not fair!
LAURA. Then change.
HANNAH. Into what?
LAURA. I don't know. *(Beat.)*
HANNAH. Is everyone in all black outfits, or just us?
LAURA. Um, I don't know. People wear brown too. I'm pretty sure. Earth tones. *(Pause.)*
HANNAH. Is our age group expected to wear dark sunglasses? Cuz I only have pink ones and purple ones and teal ones.
LAURA. Well, tough.
HANNAH. My new tortoise-tee has some black in the trim. Can

I wear that?

LAURA. Why are you asking me?

HANNAH. Well who am I supposed to ask? *(Beat. Pause.)*

LAURA. OK, no. I don't think you should wear your tortoise-tee.

HANNAH. How come?

LAURA. DUH! It's COMPLETELY inappropriate!

HANNAH. How would YOU know! How would you know anything! *(Laura throws an item of clothing at Hannah.)* Ow! Bitch!

LAURA. Oh, please!

HANNAH. You hurt me!

LAURA. Stop being a baby! *(Pause.)*

HANNAH. What's she gonna look like?

LAURA. We don't have to look at her.

HANNAH. How do you know? You're older. They'll put you in front. You'll have to look.

LAURA. No they won't.

HANNAH. They'll put you in front, and they'll put me in back, with Grandma. It's no fair! She gives me dirty cough drops from the bottom of her purse. She makes that clucking sound cuz we don't know the prayers. I don't see why you get to sit in front and look.

LAURA. It's just cuz I'm older. *(Beat.)*

HANNAH. Who's gonna make me my waffle?

LAURA. Dad, I guess.

HANNAH. And my hot chocolate?

LAURA. Yeah.

HANNAH. He can't do the hot chocolate!

LAURA. He can too.

HANNAH. From scratch? No way! Mom doesn't use a mix. She starts with Ghiradelli Bitter Chocolate. I put my finger in it once and it was like dirt. Dog crap. It was awful tasting. You have to know how to make it.

LAURA. You just mix it with sugar and milk.

HANNAH. But you have to know exactly how much. And I don't know and he doesn't know and neither do you! *(She turns and looks at Laura.)* When did you get boobs?

LAURA. Hannah …

HANNAH. When did they get so big?

LAURA. Hannah.

HANNAH. I swear you got them today! You're not supposed to have big fat boobs! *(Beat.)* Are you sexually active?
LAURA. Where did you hear that?
HANNAH. When are we going back to school?
LAURA. I don't know.
HANNAH. Are you going to cheer practice? *(Beat.)*
LAURA. I don't know.
HANNAH. Are you gonna be in the game one greeting cheer?
LAURA. Of course!
HANNAH. Not if you don't go back to practice! *(Beat.)* If you're not in the game one greeting cheer, you can forget about being a starter this year. You're gonna be an alternate again, senior year, the last cheer year of life!
LAURA. That's none of your goddamn business!
HANNAH. Are you still going to work?
LAURA. I don't know! *(In silence they pick up brushes and brush their own hair. Lights shift revealing their dad, Phil. Somewhere else. Just looking out.)* Everybody's gonna be looking at us! It'll be sort of like a pep rally, but quiet, and we're the pom squad. So we have to think about how we're gonna look! Come here. *(Hannah is making a mess of her hair. Laura reluctantly goes to her and begins to comb it.)*
HANNAH. When's Dad coming back?
LAURA. I'm not sure.
HANNAH. I heard something from the other room. When Dad was calling everybody. He said something about the size of the hole it made in her head. When her head hit the ground! *(Panic. Builds.)* Are we gonna have to look at it? The hole? *(Laura accidentally pulls Hannah's hair.)* Ow! Bitch!
LAURA. Fine! Then do it yourself! *(Laura moves away from her.)*
HANNAH. Do you think the stuff from my old room is still in the storage facility? I'd like to get that mobile back I had over my bed. That circled around and played those stupid tinkly little songs? I bet Dad has it logged on a list on his computer. I want to get it back! *(Beat.)* You have humongous disgusting tits. *(They hold a tableau. Hugging themselves. Lights shift. Phil, still in a pool of light. A cop speaks to him, in voice-over.)*
COP. We're very sorry for your loss.
PHIL. Thank you.

COP. This is really just a technicality. We just have to clear up a few facts with you regarding your whereabouts on the afternoon of the eighth of September.

PHIL. I was at work.

COP. You were at your office.

PHIL. No. I was out in the field, actually. At the survey site.

COP. So you were out at the wetlands. *(Beat.)*

PHIL. No. *(Beat.)*

COP. To have to answer these questions, sir, in light of your loss, must be very difficult, but we do need to verify —

PHIL. No. It's not that. It's that ... *(Beat.)* They are not "wetlands." That's a myth generated by the environmental lobby. It is a man-made bog. We're draining and reclaiming it for the community.

COP. OK.

PHIL. I was doing a check-in at the survey site on Camino Del Mar. It was only the first day of our hydrology study and we're already at two weeks to public review. I walked the site, did a quick touch base with the team heads. Routine stuff. *(Beat.)* And when I got back to the office, the message light was blinking. So I pressed the button and the machine said, "YOU HAVE ONE NEW MESSAGE." And it was my daughter Laura's voice. "Dad come home. Mom is dead." Then there was a very long beeping sound and the machine said, "TO ERASE PRESS TWO. TO SAVE PRESS THREE." *(Beat.)* You don't think you're ever gonna hear that. *(Pause.)*

COP. Sir, was your wife an avid jogger?

PHIL. She was very physically fit.

COP. She jogged routinely?

PHIL. After breakfast. That was her morning.

COP. And she was aware of the dangers of jogging on the old bluff road? The traffic diversions being caused by the Surfswell Plaza Freeway Project?

PHIL. We were always telling her. I would tell her.

COP. Because where her body was found ... she was jogging in a very dangerous place. Any car doing fifty, particularly if they're not local and they don't know how to take the Caminito Curve ...

PHIL. I told her! I bought her a treadmill and put it in the atrium where there's plenty of natural light. But she wanted to jog on the old bluff road. Look out at the ocean. I told her she was nuts. The traffic, the erosion. *(Beat.)* She's the one who found this neighborhood. We drove up the coast looking for a place to live, when she was pregnant with our first child. A place with ocean views, reasonable seafood restaurants, and good schools. Eighteen years, we've been here. That's a lifetime in this community. Got in on the first tract development they cut into the hill. The iceplant hadn't grown over the retaining walls yet. The cement dividers were still soft. We got a Spanish stucco ocean view unit for forty-five thousand dollars. It's worth ten times that now, as a tear-down! *(Beat.)* She planted this eucalyptus seedling when we got here. It's a huge thing now. Towering over the breakfast nook. Dropping leaves into our jacuzzi. *(Beat.)* I tried to tell her that things had changed.

COP. I think we have the information we need to pursue the matter. Thank you for coming in. I want to tell you how our hearts and prayers go out to you and your family.

PHIL. We're Jewish people actually. My family. We don't practice, not since we moved here. But just so you know, if you are gonna pray. Pray Jewish. *(Lights shift. The sound of the freeway.)*

Scene 2

Laura's house. Laura is sorting through her dead mother's clothes with her dad.

LAURA. We're out of stuff. *(Phil holds up a hat.)*
PHIL. Keep?
LAURA. I don't know.
PHIL. Give away?
LAURA. I guess. *(Beat.)*
PHIL. What stuff?
LAURA. Stuff me and Hannah eat! Like, food!
PHIL. Didn't people leave all that ...

LAURA. It's weird casseroles. And like, pies. It's not stuff we eat. *(She holds up a jacket. He points to a pile. She throws it in.)*
PHIL. Well, then, you'll need to go to the market, I guess. Can you do that?
LAURA. Yeah.
PHIL. You know what to get?
LAURA. I used to push the cart sometimes. I know her pattern.
PHIL. What was it?
LAURA. What?
PHIL. The pattern.
LAURA. Just her way of going! The order of things?
PHIL. What order? What order was it?
LAURA. It was just the way she went, that's all. Produce, dairy, frozen stuff. Bread, drinks, check out. And she tells Hannah "NO!" when she picks up a Snickers and then she pays, and that's all.
PHIL. How are you gonna pay?
LAURA. With the ATM card.
PHIL. You know the code?
LAURA. Yeah.
PHIL. How do you know the code?
LAURA. She told it to me.
PHIL. She did?
LAURA. Yeah. *(Beat.)*
PHIL. So you'll go to the market, and you'll get what she got. And you'll make something. You'll do that chicken she does.
LAURA. With sun-dried tomatoes?
PHIL. That's the one.
LAURA. I don't know how to do that.
PHIL. Why don't you look at her cookbooks, and figure that one out.
LAURA. She didn't use cookbooks.
PHIL. Well then just figure it out, somehow, and we'll sit down to a nice family dinner. I think it's important that we do that. For Hannah.
LAURA. Can't we just order something?
PHIL. No.
LAURA. But, that's gonna take all afternoon, and I just —
PHIL. You just what? *(Laura holds up a shirt to her chest.)*

16

LAURA. Keep? *(Phil looks at it for a long beat. A memory. He touches the shirt.)* Keep or give away? *(He smooths the shirt over Laura's shoulders.)*

PHIL. Looks like you could wear this one. *(Beat. Laura pulls away.)*

LAURA. Can't we get a nanny?

PHIL. I don't want some person in our house.

LAURA. What if she was here after school, only?

PHIL. I don't want a stranger here that I don't know.

LAURA. What about Grandma?

PHIL. Your grandmother lives far away from us, and it's going to stay that way. *(Beat.)*

LAURA. But I want to go to back to my work.

PHIL. You don't have to work! We've told you that.

LAURA. I like my work.

PHIL. You need to be here.

LAURA. But ...

PHIL. But, what?

LAURA. I want to go back to cheer practice.

PHIL. What?

LAURA. If I don't go back to practice now I won't learn the game one greeting cheer and if I don't know the game one greeting cheer they'll cut me and I'll never cheer varsity!

PHIL. Varsity? For jumping up and down?

LAURA. That's not what we do!

PHIL. You jump up and down ... and you yell?

LAURA. That's not what cheerleading's about! *(Laura opens the bottom drawer — the lingerie drawer. She holds up a sexy black night-gown. They freeze. A long sad silence. Phil takes the nightgown and lays it gently on the bed.)*

PHIL. Your mother was planning a family trip to Israel. You didn't know that. After the project, she wanted me to take the family on a trip to Israel. I said, are you nuts? The violence, the heat. But she said, no. Not by the coast. The coast is temperate and mild. Like here. Which makes a lot of sense for the promised land. *(Beat.)* I have to work very hard and very late until the freeway opening. The project is at its most critical phase and your little sister and I will need you here!

LAURA. The freeway blows! Everybody says! It's gonna destroy

17

natural resources!

PHIL. Do you have any idea what kind of population growth our county has seen in the last ten years? If we don't make a freeway to accommodate the Surfswell Plaza congestion then before long, every four-by-four in the Inland Empire is gonna be gunning through our formerly walkable and charming downtown shopping district. You couldn't park on Caminito Del Mango and walk to Krissie's muffins without taking your life into your hands! And before we know it, they'll start bringing their inner tubes and their boom boxes full of John Cougar Mellencamp to our beaches. You won't be able to lay out on the sand anymore without some morbidly obese family eating their surplus cheese sandwiches and having a domestic dispute! Everything we have would be ruined! *(Beat.)*

LAURA. Krissie's Muffins is already closing. The plaza has a Breads Etc. megastore! *(Pause.)*

PHIL. I don't want you doing things. I want you here. *(Lights shift.)*

Scene 3

Sound of a blender. Then two. Then six. Then all the blenders of the southland, whirring at top speed. Lights up on the smoothie shop. Laura with her hand on the top of a blender. Her body shakes. It stops.

LAURA. 'K. First you add the Basic Boost. *(Adds something to the blender. Puts on the top. Loud blending sound again. Her body shakes. It stops.)* Now the All-Pro Protein. *(Adds something.)* Then, ask if they've tried any of our "Smoothie Madditives" which are: Mood Lift, Memory Boost, Energina, Youth Jolt, and Mega-Cleanse. Then, tell them about this week's promotional madditive, which is — *(Checks a list)* Moby Thick! — a fiber blend made from the baleen of humpback whales whose healthful benefits have been enjoyed by the Inuit people for centuries. And we guarantee these

18

whales died naturally by old age and not poaching or disease. *(She considers this a beat, then shakes it off.)* Then, they pick their fruit. Oh, you're supposed to try to push the new fruits. Otherwise, people will just get like, strawberry and banana. There's a new hybrid of kiwi and cassava melon — it's called Kissava — and it has twice the mineral content of an average serving of fruit. *(Beat.)* You're supposed to say that. Oh, and the cool thing is, no matter what you put in, you always add our special smoothie starter at the end. That way, the color always comes out the same. The healthful rosy flush that customers want. If you forget this final additive the color will be a greyish brown. And when they see it, they won't like it. *(Beat.)* Oh, and if you mess it up, just throw it away and do it over. We never run out of anything. Somebody comes in at night and stocks it all, I guess. *(Pause.)* I don't know how. Some of the stuff is like, really heavy. *(Considers a long beat, then goes on.)* 'K, that's it. That's all you need to know. *(Beat.)* Now blend! *(Noise of a thousand blenders. Lights shift.)*

Scene 4

Transition. Cheer practice. Stomping sounds. The cheerleaders explode onto stage, then come together into a Fosse clump and hit a solid frozen pose. Tight. Serious faces. On another beat, they smile. On another beat, they sneer. On another beat, they do a sexy, wild dance. Then they do a bunch of military-style moves.

CHEERLEADER #1. READY?
CHEERLEADERS. OK! *(Beat. A cheer.)*
    GO!
    FIGHT!
    WIN!
    GO!
    GO! FIGHT! WIN!

(Music stops.)

LESLIE. I have an idea!

CHEERLEADER #1. Excuse me!

LESLIE. I made something up.

CHEERLEADER #2. YOU made something up?

LESLIE. Well, since we don't have Laura anymore, I thought I would make up a new game one greeting cheer, that works without her. And I thought I would up the ante a little too, while I was at it.

CHEERLEADER #3. Up the what?

LESLIE. Make it BETTER! 'K?

CHEERLEADER #1. OK, Leslie. Show us your cheer.

LESLIE. *(Builds ferociously.)* Thanks. OK. It goes, "Seagulls, DOMINATE! This is our year — make it great! Victory! Is our fate! Our battlefield is your booty. Our field is your behind. We'll stomp you down we'll beat your butts I SAID WE'LL BLOW YOUR MIND!" *(Beat.)* And on "mind," we're gonna basket toss Katie into a double "V" toe-touch jump, and while she's in the air, we're gonna turn out and do a fully extended "happy face with jazz hands," then melt into a sexy face pivot, catch Katie, slap back to buckets, smile, sneer, and then here's the thing ... *(Beat.)* Simultaneous standing back tucks. *(Cheerleaders gasp.)* 'K?

CHEERLEADER #2. Um, what?

LESLIE. Simultaneous standings! It's de rigueur among competitive squads. *(Beat.)* And we could get butt patches that say stuff when we flip! *(Beat.)* 'K? *(Silence. No one responds.)*

CHEERLEADER #1. *(Light, friendly.)* Um, I'm glad you took the initiative to make up a cheer, but ... standing back tucks? Isn't that where you like fling your body upside down? Backwards?

CHEERLEADER #3. You basically throw your head on the ground. *(Beat.)*

LESLIE. Yes, it'll take some commitment. But together we can conquer it. *(Beat.)* And it'll be 32-carat when we nail it, I swear to you. *(Beat.)* 'K? *(Silence. Laura walks out from behind the pack of cheerleaders. She is not in her practice uniform. Everybody except Leslie sees her. They freeze. It's her first time back since it happened.)* I said ... 'K? *(Silence.)* You guys? *(Beat.)* 'K? *(The cheerleaders exit, freaked. Laura slowly approaches Leslie. Long pause.)*

LAURA. 'K. *(Lights shift.)*

Scene 5

Laura's house. Hannah is hysterical.

HANNAH. A chainsaw! With a chainsaw!

LAURA. What kind of a chainsaw?

HANNAH. That kind that makes the loudest noise ever and cuts down trees! He was cutting it down!

LAURA. When did he do this?

HANNAH. He said, "It could fall down on the house at any time." He said we were in danger. He said, "They're notoriously shallow-rooted trees." He researched it.

LAURA. What are?

HANNAH. Eucalyptus!

LAURA. Where did he get a chainsaw?

HANNAH. We had one in the garage.

LAURA. We did?

HANNAH. Under stuff. Under late night television fitness machines. Recycling. It was there. *(Beat.)* It was SO LOUD! Like somebody making a smoothie out of a tennis racket! It sounded AWFUL! *(She cries.)*

LAURA. He cut down our eucalyptus tree?

HANNAH. It tipped over our property line and onto the Stevensons' sports court. And that's grounds for a lawsuit! And then he just sat down on the stump and he goes, "It's over. It's over. It's over."

LAURA. Like that?

HANNAH. Three times. *(Beat. Then hysterical.)* We have a murdered mom!

LAURA. It's not murder!

HANNAH. Murder happens here!

LAURA. It's not murder! It was a hit and run. A terrible accident.

HANNAH. But they said it was a death trap and she jogged right into it!

21

LAURA. Sh!

HANNAH. What killed her?

LAURA. Just, a car. Hit and run.

HANNAH. But what EXACTLY? What?

LAURA. The impact, I guess.

HANNAH. How? Did it crush her heart? Did her brain just pancake? Did it make a hole that made all her living parts come out and mix with the dirt in the road?

LAURA. No! She died instantly. She just closed her eyes and died.

HANNAH. Whose fault is it?

LAURA. It's not anybody's fault. It was an accident.

HANNAH. There's faults! There's always faults! Underneath us! Cracks in the earth that open up and shake and swallow things. *(Beat.)*

LAURA. Sh, no. She closed her eyes and died.

HANNAH. How do they make asphalt?

LAURA. I don't know.

HANNAH. Cement is one thing, and asphalt is a lot of things mixed, right? Gravel and cement and tar. How do they mix things that are so hard?

LAURA. They have to heat them up I guess.

HANNAH. When they're hot they're soft, and when they get cold they're hard!

LAURA. That's right.

HANNAH. Our mom got crushed in the road!

LAURA. No! Sh. Come here. It's okay. Come here. *(Hannah falls heavily into her arms. Laura rocks her, strokes her hair. She sings the tune their mother used to sing to them. Hannah begins to calm.)* Sh. I'm here. I'm here. *(Lights shift.)*

22

Scene 6

Cheer practice has just ended. It's just Laura and Leslie.

LESLIE. I'm so glad you're allowed to come back to practice now.
LAURA. Thanks.
LESLIE. We missed you. *(Beat. Serious.)* I missed you.
LAURA. I wasn't sure you knew me.
LESLIE. We're squadmates!
LAURA. Well, yeah, but. I just didn't think you could really tell me and Laura Lesterson apart sometimes.
LESLIE. Well, now I can. 'K?
LAURA. 'K.
LESLIE. I'm pregnant.
LAURA. Oh.
LESLIE. Jeremy Ashton, that needle dick prick wank. He said he'd pull out right away. Well so did Nixon in 'Nam!
LAURA. Who?
LESLIE. You know, Jeremy. He drives the magenta Jetta! We hooked up at Kira Kartanian's Labor Day weekend pool party on Friday night and then we cruised to TJ on the school day off. *(A shameful secret.)* His mom LIVES in the Seabluff Bungalow Suites. I dumped him the day after. And Stacie said he bragged to the whole longboarding team that I swallow. *(Beat.)* And then I skipped my p and now I have to get the dustbuster.
LAURA. What a jerk. Are you telling your mom?
LESLIE. She'll just be SO "unconditionally supportive." She'll just hold my hand and be all, "I remember my first abortion." And then she'll "treat me" to that stinky Iraqi facialist on Coast Highway that I HATE. And then she'll buy me a "cozy" brown sweater.
LAURA. OK.
LESLIE. That's all?
LAURA. Yeah. *(Beat.)* OK. *(Pause.)*
LESLIE. I'm just kidding. Wanted to see how you'd react. Bravo.

You were totally mellow. I knew you could be my best friend.

LAURA. I can?

LESLIE. Yes. I mean I did get pregnant last year and I got an abortion. But not by Jeremy Ashton. He asked for my number and I was like "1-800-AS IF!" *(Pause.)* I knew you were my best friend. *(Long pause. They slump down. The sound of the ocean.)* There is absolutely fucking nothing to do in this stupid boring town. *(Beat.)*

LAURA. Do you want to go shopping?

LESLIE. I was just joking about joking. I am pregnant. But you are my best friend.

LAURA. 'K. Do you want to go to the beach?

LESLIE. I'm too white.

LAURA. Me too.

LESLIE. I'm chalk.

LAURA. I'm butt.

LESLIE. Let's get smoothies.

LAURA. Had one at work today.

LESLIE. Let's get wraps.

LAURA. 'K. Have you tried the sprouted cajun?

LESLIE. I get the cumin scented barbeque tofu. No cheese no sour cream.

LAURA. They have the new ocean size sodas. We can get sixty-four-ounce Diet Cokes.

LESLIE. 'K. You work?

LAURA. Yeah. At Smooth Talk.

LESLIE. Oh. Are they hiring?

LAURA. You need to work?

LESLIE. If I want department store cosmetics! If my mom had her way I'd be the Maybelline monster that she is. I used to work at Krissie's Muffins but they're on the path of the Surfswell Plaza Freeway Project. Everything's changing you know. We can't even park our own cars at our own beach anymore! They're putting in a PAY LOT with SEVERE TIRE DAMAGE and everything. We're all getting paved right under! *(Beat.)* At RJRJ — R. J. Reynolds Junior High School where I went in Winston-Salem — cheerleading was WAY more important than it is here. At RJRJ we had a weight limit and if you exceeded it, you were dismissed in a very solemn ceremony. With paddles and everything.

LAURA. Wow.

LESLIE. But these bitches are dedicated to nothing but fear and mediocrity. Won't practice basket tossing on the quad just because it's kind of cement-y? Have they ever heard of TRUSTING their spotters!

LAURA. I couldn't more totally agree.

LESLIE. We're never gonna convince these guys to care about cheer as much as we do. Not as long as we're in the Avocado Athletic League. They just don't have our commitment to the sport. *(Beat.)* We should go to a professional cheer training program. Like the Spirit Institute of the South.

LAURA. What's that?

LESLIE. It's actual professional cheerleading. The Competitive Sport of Cheer. Cheer for cheer's sake. We're talking Bible Belt intensity not this perky coastal shit. *(Beat.)* I have a brochure. It's very compelling. They have a standing back tuck. Pre-req. It's hard core.

LAURA. Do you have a standing?

LESLIE. Not yet. Do you?

LAURA. Not yet. *(Beat.)* Wait, standing back tuck? Isn't that where you like fling your body upside down?

LESLIE. Backwards! *(Beat. Leslie approaches Laura.)* There is a stirring passage in the brochure from the founder of the institute. She went from doing a dozen doughnuts and a fistful of quaaludes a day to being the first person to execute a flying heel stretch on an all-girl competitive squad. Today, she offers the skills and experience garnered on her journey to girls like us. *(Beat.)* It's two weeks. A thousand bucks. We should go.

LAURA. To S.I.S.

LESLIE. To their winter training intensive. We'd have to nail our standings. And get the cash. We could do it. This year's spirit slogan is "BELIEVE TO ACHIEVE." And they televise the final session. Let's pick weights. I say ninety-five cuz the camera adds ten so that's really 105.

LAURA. So we should just say 105 then.

LESLIE. But the camera adds ten.

LAURA. OK, so let's say eighty-five, cuz that's like ninety-five, then.

LESLIE. Eighty-five pounds. Done.

LAURA. Um, why don't they have cheerleader anchors like they have sports anchors? People who are experts on who the cheerleaders are and what they're doing. Everyone likes to look at girls more than guys so looking at the cheerleaders at professional sports events could become like the most popular spectator sport! *(Beat.)* God, I don't usually talk so much!

LESLIE. It's called spirit! We should go.

LAURA. But we'd have to train. We'd have to get good. Maybe we should get private coaching!

LESLIE. Yeah!

LAURA. Like the little gymnasts do.

LESLIE. Yeah! But they start when they're like, three. And the good ones are all from countries with harsh dictators. But no, we have to live in "America," land of the "rugged individual!" What a fucking joke!

LAURA. We'll just have to do it ourselves!

LESLIE. My mom is part of the coalition fighting the Surfswell Plaza Freeway Project. They raised money by selling this promotional cellulite cream called "FIRM UP AGAINST THE FREEWAY." We could raise money to get a private coach to teach us our standing, and the flying stunts and the double mounts! *(Beat.)*

LAURA. Um, I heard we need the freeway. Cuz otherwise fat people are gonna clog up our charming downtown shopping district.

LESLIE. The freeway blows! It's gonna destroy natural resources! *(Beat.)* I know. I'm gonna make my mom get me fake boobs. Only instead, I'll use the money for S.I.S!

LAURA. But won't she know when you don't get the boobs?

LESLIE. I'll just tell her they're subtle. Like yours. *(Beat.)*

LAURA. I don't have fake boobs!

LESLIE. We're squadmates. You can say you had your tits done. Gillian did.

LAURA. She did?

LESLIE. Why do you think she always votes for the halter top spring uniforms? She doesn't have to worry about straps showing!

LAURA. I didn't know that.

LESLIE. You can just say!

LAURA. But I didn't! *(Beat.)* They feel fake sometimes. I swear. They're kinda hard. Kind of high up. They're like, aggressive.

(Beat.) But I swear to God they just came out of my own skin. My body just made them. Fast! *(Beat.)*

LESLIE. My mom is totally flat. That's one of the reasons I hate her.

LAURA. Yeah. *(Long pause. The sound of the ocean. Laura stares out. She closes her eyes and throws her head back. Feels it.)* Standing back tuck.

LESLIE. Pre-req.

LAURA. Hard core! *(Leslie and Laura do one loud simultaneous clap, their hands in prayer pose. They turn and stare at each other, thrilled.)* OH MY GOD! *(Transition. From the chorus, we hear "Got to go! Uh huh! Got to go! That's right! Got to go!")*

Scene 7

Laura's house. Dinner. From the outside, the chorus chants, a protest:

CHORUS. BIG N! LITTLE O! The Surfswell Freeway's got to go! Uh huh! Got to go! Say what? Got to go! *(Etc. Phil slams the window shut. Sits.)*

HANNAH. Who are they?

PHIL. They're wealthy women with nothing better to do.

HANNAH. How come?

PHIL. Because they have teenagers who … drive themselves.

HANNAH. How come?

PHIL. Because time passes! I don't know. They are bored women. They have nothing to do. So they've decided to take a swing at the freeway development.

LAURA. They're sponsored by the Earth Watch coalition. It's national.

PHIL. Is that right?

LAURA. They're a fully accredited environmental group.

PHIL. They're a bag of hammers. They've already cost taxpayers three hundred thousand dollars with this sham of a lawsuit.

They're suing on behalf of some special breed of gopher which Surfswell will make no more. Well I'll tell you something, this woman, the "leader" of the "coalition" — I'll tell you where her sympathy for the gopher comes from. Have you seen the woman's overbite? This girl could eat an apple through a picket fence! *(He chuckles. They don't. Beat.)* They are suing on behalf of some pellet crapping pests. *(Pause.)*

HANNAH. I thought ... Remember, Yosemite? When she took us there. And we stayed in a cabin. And we had that nature guide who was her old friend from her Berkeley days? Who had the longest hair ever and the guitar with stickers on it? And remember how she talked different with her old friend from her Berkeley days? She called things "far out." Remember? Well, didn't she say something like, how gophers do something super important, really? Remember?

LAURA. Pockets of air in the soil. They give the ground its very life.

HANNAH. Remember? *(Laura and Hannah share a moment.)* I like gophers.

PHIL. What's in this rice?

LAURA. I need some money. Our cheer team, we're raising money to go to this special cheer training camp. We want to get really good.

PHIL. So?

LAURA. So, I want to go.

PHIL. How long?

LAURA. Two weeks. They have a "land-a-standing-pre-req." *(Beat.)* That means something.

PHIL. What about school?

LAURA. It's two weeks.

HANNAH. *(With false innocence.)* Where's North Carolina?

PHIL. What?

HANNAH. That's where it is, right?

PHIL. It's WHERE?

LAURA. I know you think it's nothing but it's not. We really want to go.

PHIL. Who's we?

LAURA. *(Beat.)* Our squad.

HANNAH. No, it's just her. And her one friend. They're the only ones that —

LAURA. It's our squad! *(Pause. Phil takes a bite of his food.)*

28

PHIL. What's in this?

LAURA. Miso broth. I cooked it with miso broth.

HANNAH. What's a miso?

PHIL. It's related to the gopher!

HANNAH. Ewww! Laura!

LAURA. No, honey. It's made from a soybean and it's very good for you. He's teasing.

PHIL. Miso broth?

LAURA. I got it at the supermarket. They have this new "World Cuisine" section? I just, got it.

PHIL. And you put it in our rice?

LAURA. She used to put stuff in it.

PHIL. She never put stuff in it. It was rice. She made us our rice.

LAURA. She put stuff in it. You don't know. I was making it. I didn't even know I could. My hands just put in the olive oil and browned the onions and toasted the rice and then I reached up like her to the cupboard above the stove. And there was the beef broth. She used to put in a can of beef broth instead of water and it would simmer in and soften it and make it rich. That's how she did it. OK. All this time.

PHIL. I don't want it different. I liked it before. *(Long pause.)*

HANNAH. I love these wrinkly tomatoes, they're so weird. It's looks like eating your ear or something.

PHIL. Your sister wouldn't put a — wait, uh-oh, my ear is gone! Laura came in my room, while I was sleeping, and she cut it off and threw it in the pasta sauce! Oh no! *(Phil chases Hannah around the table with a sundried tomato, she squeals and laughs. They spill out into the living room. Phil returns. To Laura, final.)* Um, no. *(He exits. Sounds of chasing, playing, laughter. Laura lifts the window, we hear:)*

CHORUS. Oh yeah! Got to go! That's right! Got to go! You know it! Got to go! Now show it! Got to go! *(Etc. Lights shift.)*

Scene 8

Cheer practice.

CHEERLEADER #1. READY!
CHEERLEADERS. OK! — *(Loud clapping sound, first from the chorus, and then louder, like a hundred kids stomping in a gymnasium. Laura and Leslie stand together. The other cheerleaders surround them. Sweet, light.)*
CHEERLEADERS.
   B-E-A-G-G-R-E-S-S-I-V-E!
   SO BE!
   AGGRESSIVE!
   BE! BE!
   AGGRESSIVE!
LAURA and LESLIE. *(Loud, tough.)* AGGRESSIVE!
CHEERLEADER #1. *(Light, friendly.)* You guys, what was that?
CHEERLEADER #2. That was loud.
CHEERLEADER #3. And late.
CHEERLEADER #2. It was totally loud and late!
CHEERLEADER #1. You guys are supposed to spot.
CHEERLEADER #3. What were you guys doing?
LESLIE. We were being what were saying! FOR ONCE! *(Cheerleaders look at each other. Puzzled. Pause.)*
CHEERLEADER #1. We don't do the being. We do the cheering.
LESLIE. But —
CHEERLEADERS. Yeah?
LESLIE. I want more. *(Beat.)*
CHEERLEADER #1. It's gonna get cloudy out!
CHEERLEADER #2. Yeah, k'wee just cheer?
CHEERLEADER #3. You guys? Spot us?
LAURA. No! We're not spotting!
CHEERLEADER #1. What?
LAURA. We're not! No!

CHEERLEADER #2. Why?

LAURA. Cuz, um, I mean, oh, I'm sorry. I don't know. I'm sorry.
(Leslie glares at Laura for a long moment. Laura shrugs and joins the squad. The cheerleaders go back to building their stunt.)

CHEERLEADERS.

B-E-A-G-G-R-E-S-S-I-V-E

SO BE!

AGGRESSIVE!

BE, BE!

AGGRESSIVE!

(Laura moves into a spot position. Leslie refuses. Loud sounds of clapping, stomping. Lights shift.)

Scene 9

Lights up on Leslie's house. Smoke. Dinner.

LESLIE. You smoke!

JUDY. Smoke put food on your table.

LESLIE. Well I want boobs.

JUDY. You have boobs.

LESLIE. No, I don't!

JUDY. You've got plenty.

LESLIE. I'm a B!

JUDY. That's fine. That's good.

LESLIE. That's shit. B is for below the radar. I need a C.

JUDY. How much?

LESLIE. Five grand.

JUDY. Five grand? That's too much. It should be cheaper.

LESLIE. Well I'm sure I could get it done for a sixer of Dos Equis in a Tijuana parking lot. But do you WANT me to a look like a thrift-shop waterbed?

JUDY. It can be done for less.

LESLIE. Not with the skill I deserve and the discretion you desire.

JUDY. Discretion?

LESLIE. I'll tell unless you get me them.

JUDY. Tell what?

LESLIE. Tell why we have this pile of money now after you resigned from R.J. Reynolds. And even in a white collar prison for women, I assure you, nobody likes a tattletale.

JUDY. You are way out of line. *(Beat.)* Four grand is the going rate.

LESLIE. I've done research. It's five grand. Five installments. One thousand up front. That's less than the lease on your Lexus. All you gotta do is say yes.

JUDY. Why don't you eat?

LESLIE. You know. I hate. *(Holds up a green leaf.)*

JUDY. No daughter of MINE doesn't like cilantro!

LESLIE. I hate being in the same room as cilantro. It smells like burnt eyebrows and it tastes like potting soil.

JUDY. You're just trying to upset me. You know I chose it as the patio ground cover. Next you'll tell me bougainvillea is ugly.

LESLIE. Tacky! It looks like the front of a Mexican groomsman's polyester tuxedo shirt.

JUDY. Who taught you to be racist?

LESLIE. Grandpa! *(Beat.)*

JUDY. I bought this condo at the top of the market, bankrupted myself for you, so we could have a bougainvillea covered stucco wall and the aroma of fresh local herbs wafting in through an ocean breeze. I got us out of the dead air of the humid shitty south, and I found a house, a semi-detached home, so we could make a fresh start. *(She lights another cigarette.)* Will you please eat something tonight? At least your crust.

LESLIE. I don't eat crust anymore.

JUDY. You used to only eat the crust.

LESLIE. I'm off carbs!

JUDY. But I made the fat-free chedderella mexipizza because I thought you'd eat it. I know it's a little bland, that's why I added the cilantro!

LESLIE. I eat cheese and meat only now. No carbs, no sugar. I eat the top.

JUDY. But it's a honey corn crust, from *Sauce of the Southwest* magazine. And I used the low-fat preparation option. *(Beat.)* You used to slide off the whole top, no matter what I put on it, and just eat the bottom. Even in front of company. It looked like the underside of skin. *(Beat.)* When I had my facelift, I looked.

LESLIE. I eat the top now.

JUDY. You've become more and more like your father.

LESLIE. That's because, like him, I hate you!

JUDY. You've gotten that lip thing. That ugly lip thing.

LESLIE. It's called an adolescent sneer!

JUDY. No, it's him.

LESLIE. I smoke you know. I smoke and then I suck Certs before you get home. And I ash in your tiger orchids. That's why they've lost their spots. It wasn't Santa Ana winds. It was me.

JUDY. It's him. *(Beat.)* I spent a thousand dollars on that low fat lifestyle cooking class. And now it's "no carbs"?

LESLIE. For now. I'm flirting with the lifestyle of all engineered nutrition. Powders, bars and shakes. That's it. Laura and I are losing weight for cheer.

JUDY. Why do you hate me?

LESLIE. Because you're old and ugly.

JUDY. I'm forty-three.

LESLIE. He left you.

JUDY. He left us.

LESLIE. Get me my boobs. Or I'll go too.

JUDY. Where?

LESLIE. To my father.

JUDY. You don't even know where he is.

LESLIE. Yes I do.

JUDY. You're a little liar.

LESLIE. We have an epistolary relationship!

JUDY. You heard that on word on *Oprah*!

LESLIE. He writes me all the time. I can smell him on the paper. Obsession, for Men. I write him all about my feelings. And all about you. He loves me.

JUDY. Your father wouldn't piss on your burning ponytail! He always thought you were a worthless ugly little girl from the time you were born till the time he walked out our sliding glass doors. *(Beat.)* No offense, sweetie. He ended up hating me too.

LESLIE. You'll never fit in here, Mother. You can't master the local vernacular like I have. You've got dirt under your pastel French tips and everybody knows it.

JUDY. What do you want from me?

LESLIE. Tits. *(Lights shift.)*

Scene 10

The phone zone. Leslie and Laura talk on the phone. Late at night.

LESLIE. So?

LAURA. Yeah?

LESLIE. My mom's in.

LAURA. How?

LESLIE. Blackmail.

LAURA. What?

LESLIE. Told her I'd alert the media to her tattletaling against the tobacco company. It was such a bluff. I mean I know she's an asshole, but I wasn't sure she was a professional one. Now she's margarine on my toasted sesame bagel. *(Beat. Then angry.)* You can just say!

LAURA. What?

LESLIE. I've been let down before! You can just say you're not in anymore. I knew you couldn't cut it anyway. You're just not Ginsu, like me. YOU'RE A FUCKING BUTTER KNIFE! You believed that crap about "We're not being, we're cheering!" You swallowed their horse pill of lies!

LAURA. No, no, no. I swear. I just didn't know how to do it. To my dad.

LESLIE. I thought you were gonna cash the death card!

LAURA. I couldn't do it. *(Beat.)* He just sits in the backyard, on this stump that used to be our eucalyptus tree. I have to walk over and say "Dad, come inside. I already put the fajitas into the tortillas and they're getting all gummy." I have to make him come in and eat. Or he just sits there.

LESLIE. OK. *(Beat. Calm.)* Then, what vulnerability does your father have left? We went through everything else. What does he do for a living?

LAURA. He's a development consultant.

LESLIE. What does he do?

LAURA. He, consults.

LESLIE. Who?

LAURA. Developers!

LESLIE. Of what?

LAURA. Of, lots of stuff. Places. Things. You know.

LESLIE. No, what?

LAURA. Well, at this particular point in time, of the Surfswell Plaza Freeway Project.

LESLIE. Your dad's building the freeway over the endangered wetlands and through our second-favorite muffin place?

LAURA. He's not building it, he's consulting! He is mitigating its harmful environmental impact through the implementation of certain standards. Or something.

LESLIE. This could be perfect.

LAURA. How?

LESLIE. We find some flaw in his study, or make one up. Then we blackmail him to reveal it to the press. I'll pretend my aunt is an investigative broadcast journalist.

LAURA. What does your aunt really do?

LESLIE. She's a whore.

LAURA. Oh, OK. *(Beat.)*

LESLIE. You have to think of yourself as powerful. Like ... an interior decorator! You just fan out the fabric swatches and go, "HERE THEY ARE." *(Beat. Serious.)* You think I know how to do stuff? I don't. I just do it. *(Beat.)* Sneak over tonight and stretch my middle splits for me. And spot my standing?

LAURA. You have your standing?

LESLIE. Almost. You?

LAURA. Um. I'm closer.

LESLIE. Come over!

LAURA. I can't leave. Yet. *(Beat.)* Sometimes I wonder ... no it's stupid.

LESLIE. What?

LAURA. It's just, I wonder sometimes. Sometimes I think that I don't know what I look like. That I don't really have any … traits. That I might look at a picture I'm in and not know it's me. *(Beat.)* Ever think that?

LESLIE. You have low self-esteem.

LAURA. I do?

LESLIE. There's a whole day self-esteem seminar at S.I.S.

LAURA. Do you have low self-esteem?

LESLIE. Yes! I hate myself! Duh!

LAURA. Oh. *(Pause.)*

LESLIE. There's three kinds of cheerleaders, Laura. There's flyers, bases, and spotters. Flyers and bases make stunts. And spotters, they get to stand around with their hands up making sure Laura Lesterson doesn't fall on her tennis elbow again! Spotters. IS THAT WHAT WE'RE GONNA BE FOR THE REST OF OUR LIVES? *(Lights shift.)*

Scene 11

Lights up on dinner at Laura's house. Laura lights a candle at the empty place at the table. It burns silently. Phil and Hannah eat. Laura tries to get up the nerve to say something to her dad, but can't. Lights shift.

Lights up on dinner at Leslie's house. Leslie uses her silverware to do little cheers, while she mouths the words. Her mother eats. She looks up. Leslie continues to silently cheer. Lights shift.

Scene 12

Laura's room. Laura and Hannah on the bed. Laura sits behind Hannah, brushing her hair.

HANNAH. *(Gently.)* Ow! Bitch!

LAURA. Sorry!

HANNAH. How come it was so quiet at dinner?

LAURA. I was thinking.

HANNAH. About what?

LAURA. I have a lot of stuff to think about now.

HANNAH. Are you ovulating?

LAURA. Where do you hear these things?

HANNAH. ARE you?

LAURA. No! I don't know. Maybe.

HANNAH. I think you're ovulating. That would explain it. Can I go with you to cheer camp?

LAURA. It's not cheer camp. It's the Spirit Institute of the South.

HANNAH. Are the rest of the cheerleaders going?

LAURA. I didn't say I was going!

HANNAH. Well, are they?

LAURA. No.

HANNAH. Why not?

LAURA. Because they don't care like we do.

HANNAH. Like you and Leslie?

LAURA. Yes.

HANNAH. Are you guys same-sex lovers?

LAURA. Hannah!

HANNAH. Kelly Kembrook said you guys are total lezzies. I think it's OK if you are. I would be your ally. How come you don't hang out with any of the other cheerleaders? How come you and Leslie are never in the stunts? How come you guys are always on your knees, with your hands in the air?

LAURA. The girls on the squad are jealous of us because we have

Bible Belt intensity. They're just perky coastal pep girls who want to hang at the games to get guys. They knock us cuz we dare to care for cheer for cheer's sake, and we have our sights set high. *(Beat.)*

HANNAH. Dad wants you to start co-coaching my soccer team. She was going to.

LAURA. When?

HANNAH. Now, tomorrow. Two days a week. And he wants you to supervise my piano lesson. He doesn't want me alone with that Hungarian woman. So that's another day a week. And I might start taking classes to learn the ancient language of our people.

LAURA. Latin?

HANNAH. Hebrew!

LAURA. Where do they have Hebrew lessons?

HANNAH. At Temple Del Sol. It's the temporary temple in the coastal civic center. There's this Israeli woman, Shoshana Levis, and she's starting a Hebrew school class and Dad says I should go and learn it, and you should drive me there, and read a beauty magazine in the car until it's over, and then drive me home. Like the others.

LAURA. I don't think it's "Levis." *(Pronouncing it like the jeans.)*

HANNAH. Oh.

LAURA. I think it's "Levy." *(Rhyming with "heavy.")*

HANNAH. Oh.

LAURA. Since when are we Jewish?

HANNAH. Since ever.

LAURA. Well yeah but, Hebrew?

HANNAH. Dad says it will be meaningful to me. *(Beat.)* So that's every day of the week. That means no sneaking away to cheer any more and leaving me here to cover for you. *(Beat.)* Besides, you don't have a thousand dollars, or the balls to ask Dad for it!

LAURA. Who said it's a thousand dollars! Are you spying on me?

HANNAH. Yes. Somebody has to. Ow! You're pulling my bangs too hard!

LAURA. Sorry.

HANNAH. The mobile doesn't work anymore. The tinkle stopped!

LAURA. I'm sorry.

HANNAH. I need you to stay where you are! *(Lights shift.)*

Scene 13

Laura and Leslie at the freeway. At night. alone. Blending sounds continue, combining with the sound of the freeway. They practice. A cheer. It builds.

LESLIE. READY?

LAURA.
   OK! WE'VE GOT SPIRIT!
   YES WE DO!
   WE'VE GOT SPIRIT!
   HOW 'BOUT YOU?

LESLIE.
   WE'VE GOT SPIRIT!
   YES WE DO!
   WE'VE GOT SPIRIT!
   HOW 'BOUT YOU?

LAURA.
   WE'VE GOT SPIRIT!
   YES WE DO!
   WE'VE GOT SPIRIT!
   HOW 'BOUT YOU?

LESLIE.
   WE'VE GOT SPIRIT!
   YES WE DO!
   WE'VE GOT SPIRIT!
   HOW 'BOUT YOU?

(A loud, echoing boom is heard. Strange music. The cheer chorus, as at the beginning, in voice-over. Laura and Leslie cheer along, in a building frenzy.)

CHEER CHORUS.
   CAN YOU HEAR IT?
   CAN YOU HEAR?
   DEEP INSIDE OUR POMPOMS

SOMETHING SHUSHES WHEN WE CHEER
IN THE CRACK OF OUR LIGAMENTS
WHEN WE HIGH KICK
THE SOUND OF OUR FINGERNAILS
GROWING FROM THEIR QUICKS
OUR SHOES COULD MAKE A SQUEAK
THAT COULD SHATTER GLASS
WE COULD SHAKE THE BLEACHERS UNDER
    EVERYBODY'S ASS! *(Beat.)*
IN OUR FACE IN OUR FISTS
IN OUR KNEES IN OUR KNUCKLES
IN OUR BRAS IN OUR JAWS
IN OUR TEETH THERE ARE MUSCLES
WE COULD THROW OUR BODIES UP TOTALLY
    HIGH!
WE COULD TURN OUR SNEAKERS INTO PIECES
    OF THE SKY!

(Music stops. Freeway sounds. Pause. Laura and Leslie catch their breath, entranced. Lights shift.)

Scene 14

Sound of a thousand blenders. The smoothie shop. Laura has her hand on top of a blender. Her body shakes. It stops.

LAURA. 'K. This month's Smoothie Madditives have a spiritual theme. We have Buddhaberry, Messianic Mango and Kabbalah-Cran. *(She goes to add one. Stops. A pause.)* You're supposed know this prayer. The Kaddish? You say it at people's funerals. He was faking it. He put his head down, so the rabbi couldn't see his mouth. He didn't know the words to say. Not any of them. I could tell. He was embarrassed. There are words you're supposed to say and he didn't know them. *(Laura walks to the register and takes out a wad of bills. She counts out what she needs, looks around.)* We

40

never run out of anything here! Everything gets filled right back up. Nothing ever really goes away, cuz they just put it all back! *(Beat.)* It doesn't matter what you take away! 'K? *(Beat.)* They just refill it! *(Sound of a thousand blenders. Lights shift.)*

Scene 15

Lights up on the phone zone. Late at night. Laura and Leslie in their respective rooms. Hannah leaning against the wall overhearing. Judy and Phil in their respective beds, alone. Laura and Leslie whisper ferociously.

LESLIE. READY?
LAURA and LESLIE. OK! B-E-A-G-G-R-E-S-S-I-V-E SO BE! AGGRESSIVE! BE, BE AGGRESSIVE! *(Beat.)*
LAURA. We're going! As soon as they go to sleep. *(Pause.)*
LESLIE. Can you hear your dad sleeping yet?
LAURA. I'm not sure.
LESLIE. I hear my mom.
LAURA. She snores?
LESLIE. She just breathes. And I hear it. *(Beat.)* What killed her?
LAURA. Hit and run.
LESLIE. But what, what killed her?
LAURA. The impact, I guess. *(Beat.)* There was a logo from a car in the skin of her back. A brand name fingerprint.
LESLIE. What kind of car?
LAURA. A Lexus.
LESLIE. What do you guys drive?
LAURA. A Cherokee Chief.
LESLIE. And?
LAURA. A Lexus. *(Beat.)* I hear him!
LESLIE. Breathing?
LAURA. Snoring.
LESLIE. It's time. I told you you could do it!

41

LAURA. What?

LESLIE. Get the money! From your dad.

LAURA. Right. *(Beat.)* Got yours?

LESLIE. Got it.

LAURA. Got the brochure?

LESLIE. Zipped in my duffle!

LAURA. Got the car keys?

LESLIE. Warm in my pocket!

LAURA. Which car?

LESLIE. The Lexus. My mom can drive the Jetta for once. *(They giggle, then silence.)* Ready? *(Beat.)*

LAURA and LESLIE. OK. *(Blackout.)*

ACT TWO

Scene 1

Loud loud music. The music resolves itself into a loud loud sucking sound. Lights up. Laura and Leslie in the car. Leslie drives. They both have harnesses around their waists into which are fitted sixty-four-ounce Diet Cokes. The music stops. The loud loud sucking sound continues, then breaks into two individual sputters. Then stops. Long pause. Laura and Leslie breathe, very full of air and liquid.

LAURA. Did you know that seahorses are the only animal species in the oceanic kingdom or otherwise, in which the male carries the babies? *(Beat.)* And the males are nesters, too. They can stay on one blade of sea grass for like, three whole years. Hence, their vulnerability. *(Pause.)*
LESLIE. You're not gonna be one of those people who fills the quiet spaces with like, metaphors, are you?
LAURA. God! I was just ... thinking. *(They both slurp their drinks, then sputter to a stop. Empty. Pause.)*
LESLIE. So, what else?
LAURA. *(Pouting.)* What?
LESLIE. About the seahorses.
LAURA. Well, Chinese herbalists use their desiccated and pulverized corpses to heal many injuries and ailments. Like gout, rheumatism ...
LESLIE. What are those?
LAURA. Diseases.
LESLIE. Oh. *(Long pause.)* What else?
LAURA. That's all I remember. *(Beat.)*
LESLIE. Where are we?

43

LAURA. We're getting closer.

LESLIE. How much longer?

LAURA. *(Refers to the map.)* Like, eight inches.

LESLIE. Good. We'll be there soon.

LAURA. But in the last eight hours we went like, half an inch.

LESLIE. Laura, I'm the one who remembered to steal my mom's triple A card, I'm the one who got the maps with it, I'm the one who split the line into three's and picked the stop points. So, if you have a better plan than mine for getting us there then say so. 'K?

LAURA. Well, I got the ATM card.

LESLIE. I know, and I'm grateful for that. That was a good call on your part. *(Beat.)* What's the code? I need greens bad. Let's stop and get cash and get salads.

LAURA. Um.

LESLIE. Oh my God.

LAURA. No, I know it. I know it.

LESLIE. You don't know the fucking code.

LAURA. No, no. I knew it. I swear. Fuck.

LESLIE. We were relying on that card. I got the car, you got the cash. What the hell are we gonna do?

LAURA. I know it, I swear. Just be quiet and I'll think of it. *(Beat.)* It's my sister's middle name, no that's our security system disarmer. Shit. I know it stands for something. It's some important thing in our lives. Fuck! What is it?

LESLIE. This is just great. Great! The one thing I ask you to take care of, and you don't have the courtesy to follow through. You are totally careless, you know that? *(Beat. Stunned.)* That was my mother!

LAURA. I'm sorry, it's just that somehow it's out of my head, out here. I look out and see all these, like, the lands, and somehow, that code, just, isn't there anymore.

LESLIE. You didn't get any extra cash? No spending money?

LAURA. I just got the tuition. Eight hundreds, two fifties, and five twenties.

LESLIE. You didn't even get any ones?

LAURA. I didn't think about it.

LESLIE. What about tipping? Huh? How are we gonna tip?

LAURA. I don't think you tip at like, motels.

LESLIE. We're gonna have to live off the Mobil card.

LAURA. You got the Mobil card?

LESLIE. Yes, of course I got the Mobil card. I said I was going to, and I did. That's how I work. Great. We're going to have to eat off the gas station now. This is just great. For three days. What are we gonna eat? Microwave mini-burgers? Corn dogs?

LAURA. They have yogurts there. Sometimes.

LESLIE. Yeah, like whole fat banana flavor.

LAURA. Well they have those turkey things don't they, those triangle sandwiches?

LESLIE. You're kidding, right? Those cat food quality cold cuts, on Wonder bread, with iceberg, and mayonnaise? *(Beat.)* Why don't we just get a brick of pork lard and a couple of soup spoons?

LAURA. Well maybe we could separate the turkey, that's all, and wipe off the mayo. And just eat the slices. *(Beat.)* 'K?

LESLIE. *(Beat.)* OK. *(Long pause. They have reached an open place. There are fields.)*

LAURA. What do you think they're growing?

LESLIE. I don't know. Corn. Cotton. Hay. Something.

LAURA. Hay?

LESLIE. I don't know.

LAURA. When do they pick, you think?

LESLIE. I don't know.

LAURA. How many corns on a plant? Like three? Or like twenty? Do they rip 'em out and redo 'em every year, or do the corns just wait under the weather and come back in the sun?

LESLIE. I don't know. *(Pause.)*

LAURA. How many jog bras did you bring?

LESLIE. Eight. You?

LAURA. Eight. How many books?

LESLIE. None. You?

LAURA. One.

LESLIE. What?

LAURA. *Roots.*

LESLIE. *Roots?*

LAURA. It's African-American Week in World Lit. *(Beat.)* Have you ever tried the corn wrap?

LESLIE. Already talked about that!

LAURA. Who's your favorite trainer at Vista del Body and Soul?

LESLIE. Already talked about that, too!

LAURA. 'K. *(Silence. More fields.)* Why don't we open the windows?

LESLIE. I have the AC on.

LAURA. Yeah, but why don't we try it for a bit. Let something in. *(Leslie opens the windows. Long silence. Leslie closes the windows.)*

LESLIE. That's enough.

LAURA. What did your Dad do?

LESLIE. A spokesmodel. She sold resistance training rubber bands gym to gym. He moved away with her. He hasn't communicated with me in a calendar year. *(Long pause.)*

LAURA. Elastercizers?

LESLIE. Yeah, those.

LAURA. Nobody uses those anymore. Now that there's the new latex bands.

LESLIE. I know. They're twice as supple without compromising any of the strength. *(Beat.)* I don't know what he does now. *(Pause.)* Are we in Utah, yet?

LAURA. I haven't seen a sign.

LESLIE. My neck hurts.

LAURA. Well, pull over. It should be my turn to drive by now.

LESLIE. I'm not pulling over until we get to Utah.

LAURA. There should be an automatic neck adjustment. Our Lexus has a weight sensitive neck support.

LESLIE. So does Tracy's mom's Lexus. So does Stacie's mom's Lexus. But my mom has to get the stripped model, of course! Everybody else gets the turkey, and my mom gets the carcass! *(Beat.)*

LAURA. Is Utah … on the way to the South?

LESLIE. Look, I've skied there. Do you have a plan?

LAURA. No.

LESLIE. *(Final.)* Then, Utah.

LAURA. 'K. *(Lights shift.)*

Scene 2

Laura's house. Phil practices a speech in front of Hannah.

PHIL. It's a draft.

HANNAH. Don't apologize. Just read it!

PHIL. OK. *(Beat.)* My fellow Vista Del Solians. *(Hannah shakes her head.)* Solites? *(Hannah shakes her head.)* Soltans? *(Hannah shakes her head.)* People of Vista Del Sol? *(Hannah nods.)* People of Vista Del Sol. We live in paradise. Not a tropical place. There are no coconuts falling onto beds of moist ferns. This is a paradise of geological variety. We have high desert bluffs, deep sandstone canyons, a soft, shifting ocean floor. This is tectonic territory. There are fractures beneath it that make it violently slip, and change. Our temperamental paradise has been created by eons of constant destruction. *(Beat.)* What a shock and a revelation it must have been for our ancestors to encounter this stunning topographic diversity after crossing endless miles of flat dusty empty plains in their covered wagons. *(Beat.)* Well, not my ancestors. My ancestors were busy fleeing the Balkan pogroms.

HANNAH. Digression!

PHIL. Sorry. But nevertheless, that's why these people who talk about losing something when the Surfswell Plaza Freeway Project comes cutting through the bluff and into our town, they don't have a clue what they're talking about. Destruction is what the edge of the world is made of. These people, the "coalition," they don't understand that. What we're doing is not just important, it's inevitable. These people don't know shit about losing anything! *(He stops, agitated.)*

HANNAH. Well it's edgy.

PHIL. That last part, that's not gonna be part of it.

HANNAH. That's probably good.

PHIL. Isn't her practice over by now?

HANNAH. She probably just stayed late.

PHIL. How late?

HANNAH. She'll be back soon.

PHIL. What about dinner?

HANNAH. I'll make something.

PHIL. You will?

HANNAH. I know how. I've watched. *(Beat.)* She'll be back soon! *(Lights shift.)*

Scene 3

The Mobil station. Laura reads from the back of a bag of pretzels.

LAURA. Yep. Palm oil.

LESLIE. Jesus Christ! Even in the pretzels! And the only crackers they have are "savory flavored!" Do you know what that means, "savory flavored?"

LAURA. No.

LESLIE. Me neither, but I'm sure it's horrible.

LAURA. I think I'm starving. I think I'm really really hungry. *(Leslie grabs packages, two, three at a time.)*

LESLIE. "Covered in creamery butter." Mother of God!

LAURA. Does caffeine make you more or less hungry?

LESLIE. More. Less. More. I can't remember!

LAURA. My head is hurting. From hunger. We have to eat something here. We just have to find something that we can eat.

LESLIE. My head hurts too. But it's not hunger. I'm just pissed at you cuz you're such a useless dumbass. Just think of the goddamn code and we could at least get the dinner salad at Denny's with the dressing on the side. Can't you think of it? It has to be part of something. *(Beat.)* Caffeine Free Regular Coke. WHERE ARE WE?

LAURA. My head hurts. We have to get something.

LESLIE. What? What are we gonna get? Huh? Yes, excuse me, I'd like a tall, cold BACON CHEDDAR SODA PLEASE!

LAURA. WE HAVE TO GET SOMETHING HERE. *(Beat.)*

LESLIE. What?

LAURA. Something we want.

LESLIE. Want?

LAURA. OK. What do you feel like?

LESLIE. Feel?

LAURA. Let's just close our eyes and try to think about what we feel. What. Feels? *(Laura closes her eyes. Leslie reluctantly closes hers. Then, immediately:)*

LESLIE. I want a corn dog.

LAURA. What? *(Leslie opens eyes.)*

LESLIE. I used to eat them at the Winston County Fair, when I was a kid. With my dad. *(Beat. closes eyes again. Opens them.)* Orange soda. Do they still have that?

LAURA. Yeah. It's on the thing. It's always on the thing. It's right next to the Diet Coke.

LESLIE. I'd like the regular size one of those. The regular size.

LAURA. OK. Let's get in line. I think I might want to get us another map. I think there might be a better map than the one we've got. I'm gonna take a look. *(Lights shift.)*

Scene 4

Hannah standing in a pool of light. A cop speaks to her in voice-over.

COP. We're very sorry about this.

HANNAH. OK. Can I go now please?

COP. I'm sorry, but I need to clarify, you said, she …

HANNAH. I just said they take things more seriously than the other girls.

COP. Like what?

HANNAH. Like cheer! She said they take it more seriously than

49

the other girls, that's all.

COP. Did she say why?

HANNAH. She said that the other girls are interested in the football guys and they're not. They're interested in achieving together.

COP. Did she say what they were interested in achieving?

HANNAH. Cheerleading! They were interested in achieving in cheerleading!

COP. I'm sorry. What does that mean?

HANNAH. They were sick of how mediocre their peers were. She wanted to go to a better place.

COP. Did she use those words — "a better place"?

HANNAH. Yeah. Can I go now? Cuz, my friend's mom is taking me home.

COP. Did she make any other comments that you thought were a little strange?

HANNAH. Strange?

COP. Did she say anything about her connection to Leslie? Did she use any other words that you might remember?

HANNAH. Other words?

COP. Like, "love" or ...

HANNAH. OH! You think this is some kind of inscrutable sapphic suicide pact? *(Beat.)*

COP. How old are you?

HANNAH. Look, she and Leslie are ... different. The other cheerleaders don't ever invite them to their pre-parties. They don't ever get to stand in the middle. They're terminal flanks. And they always carry other people's megaphones to the cars after the games. They call them the spot sisters, cuz they never fly or base. They're never allowed to call a cheer. I listen to them talk on the phone. I hear what they say to each other. I take my hair dryer and stick it up to the wall. The heat coils conduct vocal sound waves with surprising clarity. Sometimes it's so quiet, for so long. And sometimes it's just like hours of "uh huh," "uh huh" and "totally." And sometimes they say things that are very frightening indeed.

COP. Hannah Rachel Green, your sister has committed theft. Do you know where she is?

HANNAH. You know how if you look at a picture just one year later, you can look back and see exactly what kind of haircut you really had? Well that's what I think she's doing. But with space instead of time. *(Beat.)* I'm eleven years old.

Scene 5

Motel room. Leslie is alone. The TV flickers in her face. Rhythmically, every six seconds, she laughs along with a laugh track, then stops. Every fourth time, she sighs. Then the laugh track stops. She still laughs, every six seconds, three more times. Then sighs. Laura enters, slamming door behind her, and stands, triumphant.

LESLIE. What did you say?

LAURA. It's done.

LESLIE. Yeah?

LAURA. It totally worked.

LESLIE. What did you say?

LAURA. You don't have to worry about it. I took care of it.

LESLIE. Well I'd like to know the plan. What did you tell the guy?

LAURA. I told him you were pregnant and that my mom died and I totally cried, I couldn't believe it, I was just crying and crying. I think he just wanted me out of there. I said our dad was coming tomorrow and paying and couldn't we just stay here till he came tomorrow.

LESLIE. You played the death card.

LAURA. Yep.

LESLIE. He bought it?

LAURA. Cash and carry baby! Look what they had in the lobby! *(She holds up a Twinkie.)*

LESLIE. I can't believe they didn't insist on an imprint. Don't they have to have an imprint? Isn't there some kind of law? The center of a Twinkie is made with lamb lard! *(Laura devours the Twinkie.)*

LAURA. This is the best best food I've ever had. Why haven't I had this before? This is … exquisite.

51

LESLIE. What if they catch us?

LAURA. We sleep and we scram!

LESLIE. But ... did you look at that man in the lobby? He had more piercings than teeth!

LAURA. We have to keep going. *(Beat.)* I'm cold.

LAURA. Shh, it's gonna be okay. Here. *(Laura throws a sweater at Leslie.)*

LESLIE. Ow! Bitch!

LAURA. I'm sorry.

LESLIE. You hurt me!

LAURA. I'm sorry, shh ...

LESLIE. I don't like it here.

LAURA. Shh. It's gonna be okay. Just, shhh ... .

LESLIE. I don't want to wear this stupid fucking sweater!

LAURA. Be quiet!

LESLIE. I hate being away from my stuff!

LAURA. Shh! Just be quiet, OK! Just, shh!

LESLIE. I want to go home be with my stuff!

LAURA. Shut up.

LESLIE. I HAVE A CORN DOG INSIDE ME. I WANT TO GO HOME!

LAURA. I SAID, SHUT UP! *(Lights shift.)*

Scene 6

Laura's house. Phil and Judy sitting in the living room, where nobody ever sits. Judy has tea, Phil doesn't.

PHIL. It's not too strong?

JUDY. It's fine, thank you.

PHIL. I don't usually make tea. Or, really, never. I've never made tea. *(Beat.)* Ever.

JUDY. Well, it's lovely. *(Pause.)* Is this one of those antique door tables? I've seen these.

PHIL. Yes, yes. It's a table made of an old door.

JUDY. They're so clever. What they think of. I have a mirror that's made from an old window. It has a sill still. *(Pause. She doesn't drink her tea.)*

PHIL. You're sure that's not too strong —

JUDY. No, no it's just right. *(Beat.)* What kind is it?

PHIL. Um, Chinese. I believe. Or Irish. No, it's Indian. Well, it's from somewhere else, I can't remember.

JUDY. Well it's lovely.

PHIL. We have so many teas.

JUDY. Then this was a very nice choice. *(Pause.)* What do you do for a living, Phil?

PHIL. I am an environmental impact consultant.

JUDY. Oh! *(Beat.)* What is that exactly?

PHIL. I consult on issues involving the impact to the environment of various development projects. And yourself?

JUDY. I was a consultant, too. A marketing consultant for a large corporation in the south. You know, there's a familiar smell here.

PHIL. I'm sorry.

JUDY. No, no. It's not an odor. It's not unpleasant at all. Just, a smell. That's familiar. That's all. *(Beat.)* I'm sorry. Sometimes I just say things. *(Pause.)*

PHIL. The girls —

JUDY. Yes.

PHIL. What are we going to do? *(Lights shift.)*

Scene 7

Motel room. Laura and Leslie stand next to twin beds, holding their thin motel bedspreads.

LAURA. Just pull it off.

LESLIE. Won't we be cold?

LAURA. You don't sleep with these. They're universally yucky.

Just strip em off.

LESLIE. But I'll get cold.

LAURA. You should have brought more sweaters.

LESLIE. How many did you bring?

LAURA. Five.

LESLIE. How did you get five sweaters in your bag?

LAURA. I made it a priority. It's cold in other places.

LESLIE. There's no way you fit five sweaters in that one bag.

LAURA. Yes I did. *(Beat.)* I left my whole hair care product pouch at home. All of it. Conditioner, retexturizer, straightening balm, pommade, paddle brush, round brush. Comb. It was so heavy. So I chucked it onto my comforter. *(Beat.)* Tomorrow I'm gonna have to use whatever complimentary product they have in the shower here. I'm gonna have to just wash it and let it be. *(Beat.)* I have no idea what it is going to actually look like. *(Beat.)* Now stuff the spreads in the corner and help me move the twins to the wall. Let's spot each other's standings.

LESLIE. But this carpet ...

LAURA. So?

LESLIE. It's like, government surplus.

LAURA. Yeah?

LESLIE. It could sand our faces off. *(Beat.)*

LAURA. In the tuck section of the brochure, it describes how a girl landed face first trying to nail her standing, and she swelled so high she couldn't see for a week. Now help me.

LESLIE. You don't have any hair product?

LAURA. Not an ounce.

LESLIE. But I have coarse, dry chemically treated hair and you have limp, fine oily hair so you can't even borrow mine! There's a whole day competitive grooming seminar at S.I.S. It's a big part of the point system if you wanna win the spirit stick at the final award ceremony. You're gonna look, I don't know what you're gonna look like!

LAURA. So?

LESLIE. We'll it's just ... I think maybe we should turn around and go home. My mom ...

LAURA. Yeah?

LESLIE. She's probably freaking by now.

LAURA. You hate her.

LESLIE. Well yeah, but …

LAURA. There's a picture in the brochure of a girl named Jolene. She and her team just won the all-girl squad professional nationals. She's the only one smiling with a closed mouth. Why? Because in the first flying stunt her mounter kicked her coming down from a heel stretch and knocked her two front teeth clean out. They flung across the gym like a couple of peppermint Chiclets. And while her mouth was welling with blood, Jolene nailed that routine to the final tumbling pass. She took that intensity and used it. *(Pause. A plea.)* Remember?

LESLIE. Yeah. It's just that she's my mom.

LAURA. And I'm your squadmate. I'm squatting for my standing. Spot me? *(Laura turns and squats into a prep position for a standing back tuck. Leslie doesn't move. Lights shift.)*

Scene 8

Laura's house.

JUDY. Do you sit in this room a lot?

PHIL. It's the living room.

JUDY. But do you really, LIVE here?

PHIL. The TV's in the other room.

JUDY. So for you this is sort of a, parlor.

PHIL. I suppose.

JUDY. That's what I would call it. This is lovely. Your house. I enjoy this whole development. I have a friend in this subdivision with this very same model of home. I enjoy her. Her living room looks much smaller than this. But she has a tendency to over-furnish.

PHIL. Actually, this area is unique in that the homes, although built in a tract style, are each, in themselves, uh, unique. It's unique in that way. And they're unusually large.

JUDY. Yes, it's very spacious here. *(Beat.)* My friend actually uses this as an office.

PHIL. Really?

JUDY. Yes. It's an unconventional choice. But she runs a gift placement service out of her home so she likes an open office area.

PHIL. Where is her living room?

JUDY. Right through that hall and to the right.

PHIL. That's my office!

JUDY. Isn't that funny? Opposites. *(Beat.)* She says she likes the living room to feel confined. Makes her feel like she's in the mountains. *(Pause.)*

PHIL. Does your daughter cook?

JUDY. Leslie! My daughter wouldn't know a saucepan if you used it to split open her tiny little head!

PHIL. Does your daughter, eat?

JUDY. None of them eat today. Don't you watch prime-time news magazines? They all "suffer" from low self-esteem. I try to work around it. Does yours puke? Now that I won't tolerate. Vomit erodes the porcelain. I have a friend with four teenage daughters and she has had to revarnish their toilets every summer. *(She notices the silver family picture frames on a piece of furniture. She stops to look. She puts down her tea cup. Beat.)*

PHIL. Yes. *(Beat.)*

JUDY. I used to have a deep fat fryer. I put everything into that. I'd make tempura and serve it with chop suey and water chestnuts. I'd have to slap her little hand cuz she'd try to eat it off the serving platter. I remember that deep bubbling sound. The oil sound. I haven't heard that in years. That was just their favorite thing. They just loved my Oriental night. *(Beat.)* I had a husband at the time.

PHIL. The neighbors sometimes make bacon. We can smell it from our breakfast nook. They're from Chicago. It reminds me of grad school. *(Beat.)* I have a Masters. In public policy.

JUDY. Oh. *(Beat. A sound. They both jump.)* Was that?

PHIL. No. Just the security system. Every few hours it checks on us. It beeps. How did I let this happen?

JUDY. We're doing everything we can. You made sure the ringer's on "HIGH?"

PHIL. Yes.

JUDY. We're doing everything we can. *(Pause.)* There's that smell

again. What is it? It's so familiar. But I can't quite place it. *(Long beat.)*
PHIL. Eucalyptus.
JUDY. Eucalyptus! *(Judy looks out the window. Sees the stump.)* Oh!
PHIL. I had to cut it down. It was time.
JUDY. Oh yes. They can fall right onto the house at any time. They're supposed to be very shallow-rooted trees.
PHIL. That's what I've heard too. *(Lights shift.)*

Scene 9

The car. Laura drives. Her hair is wild.

LESLIE. We give the money back. And say sorry.
LAURA. No!
LESLIE. It'll be snap crackle pop! I give the money back to my mom, and you give the money back to your dad, and we just cry, and say that our blood sugar was low, and our hormones were high and ... we were menstruating, and all that blood loss was really depleting our ethical stores. We play the period card!
LAURA. We're not going back! *(Beat.)*
LESLIE. What about the groundbreaking? Aren't you supposed to be there? Don't you have to be there, for your dad?
He needs you there. *(Beat.)* You're going ninety! You're not supposed to go ninety!
LAURA. Look, if we're gonna get into an accident, we might as well get into a big gnarly one and die. If we're gonna go, we're gonna go SMOOTHIED! NO TRACE!
LESLIE. Please slow down! I'll be your best friend!
LAURA. You ARE my best friend.
LESLIE. Fuck. *(Beat.)* You're going a hundred! I don't think Lexuses go a hundred! It's gonna break!
LAURA. You can go a hundred and fifty in a Lexus and not feel a thing! IT'S A LUXURY SEDAN! *(Beat.)*
LESLIE. OK, this isn't cheer any more.

57

LAURA. This is just starting to be cheer!

LESLIE. I don't know who you are. *(Beat.)*

LAURA. Know what? I didn't get the money from my dad. I stole it. From the Smooth Talk smoothie shop. I committed an actual crime. With actual consequences.

LESLIE. You stole?

LAURA. You blackmailed!

LESLIE. Yeah, my MOM! You stole from one of the pillars of the community!

LAURA. You talk a lot of shit. You know that? *(A scary pause.)*

LESLIE. You STOLE?

LAURA. Yep. I have focus and intensity!

LESLIE. You don't even have your standing!

LAURA. Yes I do!

LESLIE. You threw yourself onto the bed.

LAURA. I am so close! We just have to "Believe to Achieve!"

LESLIE. We also have to be able to do it, though. And we can't. We can't do standing back tucks. Our CARTWHEELS are for shit! We don't weigh eighty-five pounds! And, your hair! It's like, alive! It's like a ... living thing! *(Laura screeches to the side of the road. Stops.)*

LAURA. I'm doing it. I'm showing you. I can. You watch. *(Lights shift.)*

Scene 10

Laura's house. Phil, Judy, and Hannah in the family room.

HANNAH. Theft.

PHIL. What?

HANNAH. That's what he said. Grand theft. *(Beat.)* He knew my name. He pulled right up after soccer practice and it was so embarrassing. I died. Crishelle Kravitz' mom was taking me home and she had to wait! He talked to me against his car. He said he

58

needed to talk about my sister. Laura. And he knew my name. He had three long hairs gooed on the shine of his head.

PHIL. He said, theft?

HANNAH. Grand or petty or something. He said theft.

PHIL. What did you tell him?

HANNAH. I just said she left. I just said what's true.

JUDY. Are you sure it was a cop?

HANNAH. Yes. He showed me his I.D. card.

PHIL. You mean badge.

HANNAH. No, it was a card. In his wallet.

JUDY. Was he driving a black and white squad car? With a light bar?

HANNAH. No, it was more like a ... Honda.

PHIL. A Honda.

JUDY. A light blue Honda sedan?

HANNAH. Yeah.

JUDY. Was it a laminated yellow card that he showed you?

HANNAH. Yes.

JUDY. *(To Phil.)* Vista Del Soldiers. The private security force. *(Back to Hannah.)* What did he say was stolen?

HANNAH. Money. He said Laura stole money from the smoothie shop. Lots of it. They're looking for her.

PHIL. Go to your room.

HANNAH. I'm in trouble?

PHIL. Go to your room. That's where you go.

HANNAH. We're supposed to have dinner.

PHIL. Oh. Well, have dinner. And then, go to your room. *(Pause.)*

HANNAH. Daddy, what does this mean? *(Hannah exits. Judy and Phil face each other.)*

PHIL. Theft?

JUDY. It's not REALLY theft.

PHIL. She said — *(From outside, a muffled chant.)*

JUDY. They won't contact the police. They're at fifty percent capacity and this is the last thing they'd leak. They're looking for sushi and dry-cleaning tenants not pawn shops and check cashers. They'll handle it within the jurisdiction of the mall. You need to eat. Sit down at your table. I'll cook you something. We'll have dinner.

PHIL. I'm not hungry.

JUDY. What is that sound?

PHIL. What sound?

JUDY. From outside. It sounds like some kind of chanting. Hear that? Let me open your window.

PHIL. No! Please. I think I'm hungry after all. *(Lights shift.)*

Scene 11

The side of the road. Laura is in the prep position to do a standing back tuck. Leslie spots, tentatively.

LESLIE. Don't do it!

LAURA. I'm gonna. I know I can.

LESLIE. You're gonna get hurt!

LAURA. SO?

LESLIE. So this isn't what cheer is about!

LAURA. This IS what cheer is about. We're only seventeen years old. Seventeen! We're not supposed to have to take care of other people. We're not supposed to have to drive them to their piano lessons and their Hebrew lessons and make them their chicken and rice! We're seventeen! We're supposed to be reckless and careless! We're supposed to do stupid dangerous shit and learn from it!

LESLIE. No we're not! Just stop it. Why don't you look around where we are right now. Look! See how it's all dead flat here? Well some of us have actually lived in shitty places like this! You've lived your whole life where it's all nice and new but we had to work our butts off to get there! We lived in places that were dead, dead flat! Like my mom. And me! *(Beat.)*

LAURA. It's not nice and new where we live! They just pave over what's there! There's big ugly holes and they pave on top of them, that's all! *(Beat.)* I'm doing it!

LESLIE. I'm not spotting! I'm not gonna spot!

LAURA. I don't need a spot!

LESLIE. Please, don't. Please? Oh my God! *(Laura preps to flip, and just at the point of no return … Lights shift.)*

Scene 12

Phil and Judy in the phone zone.

JUDY. What did they say?

PHIL. Nothing. Still.

JUDY. You're sure you have the call waiting activated?

PHIL. Judy, you've —

JUDY. Asked you that ten times already. Sorry.

PHIL. It's okay. I understand.

JUDY. They're looking. They have the number. You have call waiting. We're doing everything we can. *(Beat.)* We only have three days left you know.

PHIL. Three days?

JUDY. Until the Surfswell Plaza Freeway Project groundbreaking. The end of our town as we know it. The coalition is kicking into high gear. They're picketing the house of Mr. X, some bigwig in the project. I've got the graveyard shift tomorrow night. We all need to do our part.

PHIL. Oh God. Oh God.

JUDY. Sh, sh. *(Beat.)* I know. *(Pause.)*

PHIL. Do you like your daughter?

JUDY. No. Do you?

PHIL. No. Wait. Which one? The older, or the younger?

JUDY. The older.

PHIL. No. She scares me.

JUDY. She scares you?

PHIL. She makes me scared.

JUDY. But we love them so much.

PHIL. Yes.

JUDY. And we know them so well.

PHIL. Yes. *(Beat.)* There's something I have to tell you.

JUDY. Yes?

PHIL. I've never said it before.

61

JUDY. Yes. I know. *(Beat.)*
PHIL. But I can't. I haven't yet.
JUDY. You can. *(Beat.)* READY?
PHIL. OK! SHE'S D-E-A-D AND SHE AIN'T COMIN' BACK TO ME.
JUDY. UH HUH. THAT'S RIGHT. AND SAY IT ONE MORE TIME.
PHIL.
    MY WIFE IS DEAD
    SHE HIT HER HEAD
    I'LL NEVER SMELL HER ON MY BED.
JUDY. UH HUH. YOU GOT IT. A LITTLE LOUDER NOW.
PHIL and JUDY.
    WE GOT OUR HOUSES
    IN THE SUN!
    BUT OUR SPOUSES
    HAD TO RUN!
    WE'RE LONELY!
JUDY. SAY WHAT?
PHIL and JUDY.
    WE'RE L-O-N-E-L-Y
    AND WE AIN'T GOT NO ALIBI!
    WE'RE LONELY!
JUDY. UH-HUH!
PHIL. WE'RE LONELY!
JUDY. THAT'S RIGHT!
PHIL and JUDY. WE'RE SPENT! *(Long pause.)*
PHIL. What was that?
JUDY. A cheer.
PHIL. For what?
JUDY. For ourselves. *(Lights shift.)*

Scene 13

Lights bump up on Leslie and Laura. Laura lies face down on the road.

LAURA. I did it.

LESLIE. You fell on your face!

LAURA. I DID IT!

LESLIE. Let me see! *(Laura's head pops up. She's bloody. She spits. A gasp.)*

LAURA. OCEAN!

LESLIE. Oh my God!

LAURA. It's ocean!

LESLIE. There's road on your face!

LAURA. How could I be so stupid!

LESLIE. You're bloody!

LAURA. It's O-C-E-A-N!

LESLIE. What is?

LAURA. The ATM code! It's the ATM code! Of course she picked that, because that was her place. She used to take us there to play, and walk around, and DO stuff. Before we started just laying on the sand to get tan. There was this one time, I was throwing these rocks at a post under the old pier. They tore the old pier down. It's something else now.

LESLIE. The Seabluff Bungalow Suites. I know.

LAURA. I was throwing these rocks hard against the posts, just enjoying how it made a cracking and smacking sound. And my mom yelled at me, "Stop it!" And she grabbed me by the wrist and led me under the pier and showed me the mussels. There were mussels that made their homes there. I thought they were just shells, or rocks or something. Things. But she said, "Look! Look close!" And I saw what came out. It was little pieces of flesh. Living tissue from a living thing. *(Beat.)* I felt like a terrible awful person, the worst. But she said, it's okay. Someone just has to teach you that you have impact. Someone has to teach you about impact. *(Beat.)* We used to swim for hours in the ocean and when it got cold, we would run out and my mom would have a wide, white towel open and she would clutch us up in it and rub us warm and dry. She'd call us her baby burritos. That was before we had wraps. *(Pause.)*

LESLIE. My dad used to take me onto roller coasters. That was our thing. I would ride the scariest loopiest roller coaster when I was legally way too little. He used to call me Ironsides. That means I'm really fucking strong. *(Beat.)* Oh my God! Do you smell that?

LAURA. What?

LESLIE. Don't you smell it? *(Laura sniffs.)*

LAURA. Yeah. What is it?

LESLIE. It's tobacco! It's a crop that we grow here. In the South. I can't believe it. *(Beat.)*

LAURA. We made it.

LESLIE. Oh my God!

LAURA. Get in the car!

LESLIE. We're here! *(Lights shift.)*

Scene 14

Laura's house. Dinner. Phil, Hannah, and Judy quietly eating.

PHIL. This is lovely.

HANNAH. What is it?

JUDY. I had to work with what was here. You have quite a few sun-dried tomatoes.

HANNAH. *(Trying to revive the joke.)* Oh no! Wrinkle tomatoes! *(Phil gives her a token chuckle.)*

JUDY. They're very high in sodium. And there were quite a few dusty cans of beef broth in the back there. I used one in the rice.

PHIL. I can tell. It's very hearty.

JUDY. We almost never cook with beef any more. It's mostly

chicken and the fresh fish I get from Hattie's Heart-Friendly Butcher on Camino Del Mar. My friend Hattie opened that place after her husband had a massive infarction three years ago. That shop saved their life and their livelihood. Of course, they're right on the path of the Surfswell Plaza Freeway Project. She's the one who got me involved with the coalition to fight the freeway. It's been very fulfilling for me. *(Chanting is heard.)* There's that noise again. What is that?

PHIL. Pass the rice please.

HANNAH. You have the rice.

PHIL. Then pass something else!

JUDY. What is that sound? *(Hannah opens the window. We hear the protest.)*

CHORUS
    H! *(CLAP!CLAP! CLAP!CLAP!)*
    E! *(CLAP!CLAP! CLAP!CLAP!)*
    L! L! *(CLAP!CLAP!)*
    N-O!
    SURFSWELL PLAZA FREEWAY PROJECT *(CLAP!)*
    HELL NO! *(Etc. Hannah closes window.)*

HANNAH. My dad did it.

JUDY. Pardon me?

HANNAH. It's Dad's freeway.

JUDY. Is that so?

PHIL. I'm consulting.

HANNAH. It's my dad's project.

JUDY. You're Mr. X?

PHIL. I'm a development consultant, which means I'm mitigating its harmful environmental impact through the implementation of certain standards.

HANNAH. There's a groundbreaking ceremony in two days. Did he invite you?

JUDY. A groundbreaking?

HANNAH. Yeah. They're tenting the whole area. They're already setting up the grandstands and the carnation arch and the beer garden. There's gonna be complimentary muffins courtesy of Breads Etc. There's gonna be news vans and roving photographers and man on the street opinion polls. And my dad is gonna cut the ribbon. Aren't you Dad?

PHIL. That hasn't been determined.

HANNAH. *(To Judy.)* Did he invite you to come? *(Pause.)*

JUDY. I will be there. *(Beat.)* Hannah, more broccoflower?

HANNAH. I've consumed quite enough.

JUDY. Phil?

PHIL. Yes. Thank you. *(He doesn't take any. Lights shift.)*

Scene 15

An abandoned schoolyard. Laura and Leslie run in.

LESLIE. Nobody.

LAURA. Did you run around the back again?

LESLIE. Four times!

LAURA. Me too!

LESLIE. I looked under rocks! I looked under leaves! There's no one here.

LAURA. What happened?

LESLIE. Let's look at the brochure again. Maybe we got it wrong. *(Laura looks at the brochure.)*

LAURA. Where did you get the brochure?

LESLIE. I found it.

LAURA. Where?

LESLIE. In the library. I went to the mag rack at recess to put on some perfume from a *Mirabella*. And I saw it poking out of a shelf.

LAURA. When?

LESLIE. A while ago.

LAURA. Do you see what this says at the bottom? Right here? In solid black ink? *(Beat.)* Copyright 1971. 1971! See how the print's all weird? How the letters are like, all, flared at the bottom?

LESLIE. I thought it was retro.

LAURA. Oh my God. *(Long pause.)*

LESLIE. My mom says everything comes back. Shoulder pads, everything. She says you just keep it in your closet and you hold on tight. Cuz everything comes back! My mom says it does!

LAURA. No, it doesn't. In 1971, my mom was alive, and she's dead now. In 1971, my mother was alive, and today, she's gone.

LESLIE. But she's always in your heart.

LAURA. Is that all there is to say? Cuz that doesn't mean anything. *(She stares at the brochure)* In 1971, I wasn't even around yet. But that's when she was really alive, I think. She had a grey streak in the front of her hair. Premature grey. She had it for years until she finally got sick of the giggles and stares and she dyed it like the rest of them. I don't even remember barely. I was so little. She used to tell us things, but I barely remember and I can't ask her again! I can't say, "Hey, Mom, tell me things I never listened to! Tell me how to do things! Tell me how to bake sugar cookies so they're soft in the middle! Tell me how to sweep my hair up so it holds with just a pin. Tell me what it feels like when your water breaks and a baby comes out! I don't have anybody to tell me that! *(Laura starts to tear the brochure.)* I hate my dad! I'm sorry, but I hate him so much! How could he just keep going? I don't understand how he could just keep going! *(Beat.)* Is that what happens? You're young, and you believe in things, and then you, what? You get married, you have kids, you move into a Spanish stucco ocean view unit and you forget? One day you wear your white streak like a peacock's tail, and the next day you're letting them paint it with bleach and toner and wrap it in tin foil and sitting under a hair dryer to cook for an hour while you learn lip-lining tips from a beauty magazine! Like everybody else! When you sit under those dryer domes, you can't see or hear a thing. You just have to sit there quietly and let all that stuff soak into you. *(Beat.)* She's really kind of been gone for a long long time. *(Laura finishes tearing the brochure and starts to scatter the pieces.)* I don't want to be a dead girl. I want to be a person who's alive. *(She turns and starts to slowly walk away.)*

LESLIE. Where are you going? *(Laura turns. A beat.)*

LAURA. I'm going home. *(Lights shift.)*

Scene 16

Hannah's room. Judy sits on Hannah's bed, brushing Hannah's hair.

JUDY. They're not wetlands. That's a myth generated by the environmental lobby. It's a man-made bog. They're draining and reclaiming it for the community.

HANNAH. What about the gophers!

JUDY. There's been a gopher agreement. In the settlement. There's a gopher provision in the project!

HANNAH. What are they gonna do to them?

JUDY. They're building a temporary burrowing facility.

HANNAH. They're gonna build gopher condos?

JUDY. It's only temporary.

HANNAH. Out of what material will they build these condos? Are they gonna protest big time? Are they gonna hang my dad in effigy? Is he gonna have to testify?

JUDY. No, there's been a settlement. That means they've dropped the lawsuit. It's over.

HANNAH. They're gonna build them out of tar and gravel. The gophers have to settle for the gravel! *(Beat.)*

JUDY. Here's something I can teach you. You'll learn that you can live with almost anything. You can find a way to make it work and move on. Do you hear me? You can make it work and keep going. *(Lights shift revealing Phil, isolated in a pool of light.)*

PHIL. The bluffs crumble to the beach. The waves wash the sand away and for a while there are jagged rocks and trash all over the shore. But the city comes in with trucks and deposits a fine layer of sand over the broken glass and the discarded feminine hygiene products and replenishes the smooth recreational surface .we've come to know and rely upon. With just a little help from man, nature's cycle continues. In a year, this very ground upon which we stand will be racing with high-speed cars. Today we move forward.

68

We don't look back. We proudly pave our way to tomorrow.

Scene 17

Lights up on the groundbreaking ceremony. Phil is now flanked by Judy and Leslie and the cheerleader chorus. He holds a ceremonial shovel.

PHIL. Thank you. Thank you. I played only a small part in this. I consulted, only. But I thank you. For your support. *(He goes to dig, but stops. He can't. Judy approaches, and helps him dig. They wait for applause, none comes. They look to Leslie. She gets the crowd to applaud. By cheering. The sound of applause. Lights shift.)*

Scene 18

Lights fade out on everyone but Hannah and Laura, who stand at the beach, using their toes to write in the sand.

LAURA. What does yours say?
HANNAH. I'm not done, wait!
LAURA. Let me see!
HANNAH. Wait! There.
LAURA. What does it say?
HANNAH. You first.
LAURA. OK. Mine says, "LYING." I lied about stuff. What does yours say?
HANNAH. Forgetting. I'm afraid I'm forgetting her. I can't remember what it tasted like when she leaned over to kiss goodnight and some of her hair would get in my mouth. *(Beat.)*

LAURA. We're not gonna forget her.

HANNAH. Well Shoshana said whatever you want to wash away. You can write it. *(Beat.)* We should go! We're supposed to meet them in ten minutes. We're supposed to cheer for Dad.

LAURA. It's over.

HANNAH. What's over?

LAURA. The groundbreaking. It was over an hour ago.

HANNAH. Why didn't you take me there? We're gonna get into trouble! We were supposed to cheer for Dad.

LAURA. I kind of quit cheering. I'm gonna try to do something else.

HANNAH. What?

LAURA. I don't really know yet. What else does Shoshana say? *(Pause.)*

HANNAH. She says ... wait! Here comes a wave. *(They grab hands.)*

LAURA. Here we go.

HANNAH. Here it comes! *(Beat.)*

LAURA. Ready?

HANNAH. OK. *(As they run back, laughing, the sound of a wave crashing, then the sound of the Pacific Ocean. Lights fade.)*

End of Play

PROPERTY LIST

Pom-poms (CHEERLEADER CHORUS)
Clothing (LAURA, PHIL)
Hairbrushes (LAURA, HANNAH, JUDY)
Hat (LAURA)
Jacket, shirt (LAURA, PHIL)
Nightgown (LAURA)
Blender, additives, list (LAURA)
Sun-dried tomato (HANNAH)
Cigarettes, lighter (JUDY)
Cilantro (LESLIE)
Candle (LAURA)
Silverware (LESLIE)
Register, money (LAURA)
Harnesses, 64-ounce drinks (LAURA, LESLIE)
Bag of pretzels (LAURA)
Bags of snack food (LESLIE)
Twinkie (LAURA)
Sweater (LAURA)
Tea (JUDY)
Bedspreads (LAURA, LESLIE)
Brochure (LAURA)
Shovel (PHIL)

SOUND EFFECTS

Ocean
Freeway
Car crash
Blenders
Clapping, stomping
Loud boom
Strange music
Loud music
Loud sucking sounds and sputters
TV laugh track
Beep
Chanting
Applause
Wave crashing

NEW PLAYS

★ **MONTHS ON END by Craig Pospisil.** In comic scenes, one for each month of the year, we follow the intertwined worlds of a circle of friends and family whose lives are poised between happiness and heartbreak. "...a triumph...these twelve vignettes all form crucial pieces in the eternal puzzle known as human relationships, an area in which the playwright displays an assured knowledge that spans deep sorrow to unbounded happiness." *–Ann Arbor News.* "...rings with emotional truth, humor...[an] endearing contemplation on love...entertaining and satisfying." *–Oakland Press.* [5M, 5W] ISBN: 0-8222-1892-5

★ **GOOD THING by Jessica Goldberg.** Brings us into the households of John and Nancy Roy, forty-something high-school guidance counselors whose marriage has been increasingly on the rocks and Dean and Mary, recent graduates struggling to make their way in life. "...a blend of gritty social drama, poetic humor and unsubtle existential contemplation..." *–Variety.* [3M, 3W] ISBN: 0-8222-1869-0

★ **THE DEAD EYE BOY by Angus MacLachlan.** Having fallen in love at their Narcotics Anonymous meeting, Billy and Shirley-Diane are striving to overcome the past together. But their relationship is complicated by the presence of Sorin, Shirley-Diane's fourteen-year-old son, a damaged reminder of her dark past. "...a grim, insightful portrait of an unmoored family..." *–NY Times.* "MacLachlan's play isn't for the squeamish, but then, tragic stories delivered at such an unrelenting fever pitch rarely are." *–Variety.* [1M, 1W, 1 boy] ISBN: 0-8222-1844-5

★ **[SIC] by Melissa James Gibson.** In adjacent apartments three young, ambitious neighbors come together to discuss, flirt, argue, share their dreams and plan their futures with unequal degrees of deep hopefulness and abject despair. "A work...concerned with the sound and power of language..." *–NY Times.* "...a wonderfully original take on urban friendship and the comedy of manners—a *Design for Living* for our times..." *–NY Observer.* [3M, 2W] ISBN: 0-8222-1872-0

★ **LOOKING FOR NORMAL by Jane Anderson.** Roy and Irma's twenty-five-year marriage is thrown into turmoil when Roy confesses that he is actually a woman trapped in a man's body, forcing the couple to wrestle with the meaning of their marriage and the delicate dynamics of family. "Jane Anderson's bittersweet transgender domestic comedy-drama ...is thoughtful and touching and full of wit and wisdom. A real audience pleaser." *–Hollywood Reporter.* [5M, 4W] ISBN: 0-8222-1857-7

★ **ENDPAPERS by Thomas McCormack.** The regal Joshua Maynard, the old and ailing head of a mid-sized, family-owned book-publishing house in New York City, must name a successor. One faction in the house backs a smart, "pragmatic" manager, the other faction a smart, "sensitive" editor and both factions fear what the other's man could do to this house— and to them. "If Kaufman and Hart had undertaken a comedy about the publishing business, they might have written *Endpapers*...a breathlessly fast, funny, and thoughtful comedy ...keeps you amused, guessing, and often surprised...profound in its empathy for the paradoxes of human nature." *–NY Magazine.* [7M, 4W] ISBN: 0-8222-1908-5

★ **THE PAVILION by Craig Wright.** By turns poetic and comic, romantic and philosophical, this play asks old lovers to face the consequences of difficult choices made long ago. "The script's greatest strength lies in the genuineness of its feeling." *–Houston Chronicle.* "Wright's perceptive, gently witty writing makes this familiar situation fresh and thoroughly involving." *–Philadelphia Inquirer.* [2M, 1W (flexible casting)] ISBN: 0-8222-1898-4

DRAMATISTS PLAY SERVICE, INC.
440 Park Avenue South, New York, NY 10016 212-683-8960 Fax 212-213-1539
postmaster@dramatists.com   www.dramatists.com

NEW PLAYS

★ **BE AGGRESSIVE by Annie Weisman.** Vista Del Sol is paradise, sandy beaches, avocado-lined streets. But for seventeen-year-old cheerleader Laura, everything changes when her mother is killed in a car crash, and she embarks on a journey to the Spirit Institute of the South where she can learn "cheer" with Bible belt intensity. "…filled with lingual gymnastics…stylized rapid-fire dialogue…" –*Variety*. "…a new, exciting, and unique voice in the American theatre…" –*BackStage West*. [1M, 4W, extras] ISBN: 0-8222-1894-1

★ **FOUR by Christopher Shinn.** Four people struggle desperately to connect in this quiet, sophisticated, moving drama. "…smart, broken-hearted…Mr. Shinn has a precocious and forgiving sense of how power shifts in the game of sexual pursuit…He promises to be a playwright to reckon with…" –*NY Times*. "A voice emerges from an American place. It's got humor, sadness and a fresh and touching rhythm that tell of the loneliness and secrets of life…[a] poetic, haunting play." –*NY Post*. [3M, 1W] ISBN: 0-8222-1850-X

★ **WONDER OF THE WORLD by David Lindsay-Abaire.** A madcap picaresque involving Niagara Falls, a lonely tour-boat captain, a pair of bickering private detectives and a husband's dirty little secret. "Exceedingly whimsical and playfully wicked. Winning and genial. A top-drawer production." –*NY Times*. "Full frontal lunacy is on display. A most assuredly fresh and hilarious tragicomedy of marital discord run amok…absolutely hysterical…" –*Variety*. [3M, 4W (doubling)] ISBN: 0-8222-1863-1

★ **QED by Peter Parnell.** Nobel Prize-winning physicist and all-around genius Richard Feynman holds forth with captivating wit and wisdom in this fascinating biographical play that originally starred Alan Alda. "QED is a seductive mix of science, human affections, moral courage, and comic eccentricity. It reflects on, among other things, death, the absence of God, travel to an unexplored country, the pleasures of drumming, and the need to know and understand." –*NY Magazine*. "Its rhythms correspond to the way that people—even geniuses—approach and avoid highly emotional issues, and it portrays Feynman with affection and awe." –*The New Yorker*. [1M, 1W] ISBN: 0-8222-1924-7

★ **UNWRAP YOUR CANDY by Doug Wright.** Alternately chilling and hilarious, this deliciously macabre collection of four bedtime tales for adults is guaranteed to keep you awake for nights on end. "Engaging and intellectually satisfying…a treat to watch." –*NY Times*. "Fiendishly clever. Mordantly funny and chilling. Doug Wright teases, freezes and zaps us." –*Village Voice*. "Four bite-size plays that bite back." –*Variety*. [flexible casting] ISBN: 0-8222-1871-2

★ **FURTHER THAN THE FURTHEST THING by Zinnie Harris.** On a remote island in the middle of the Atlantic secrets are buried. When the outside world comes calling, the islanders find their world blown apart from the inside as well as beyond. "Harris winningly produces an intimate and poetic, as well as political, family saga." –*Independent (London)*. "Harris' enthralling adventure of a play marks a departure from stale, well-furrowed theatrical terrain." –*Evening Standard (London)*. [3M, 2W] ISBN: 0-8222-1874-7

★ **THE DESIGNATED MOURNER by Wallace Shawn.** The story of three people living in a country where what sort of books people like to read and how they choose to amuse themselves becomes both firmly personal and unexpectedly entangled with questions of survival. "This is a playwright who does not just tell you what it is like to be arrested at night by goons or to fall morally apart and become an aimless yet weirdly contented ghost yourself. He has the originality to make you feel it." –*Times (London)*. "A fascinating play with beautiful passages of writing…" –*Variety*. [2M, 1W] ISBN: 0-8222-1848-8

DRAMATISTS PLAY SERVICE, INC.
440 Park Avenue South, New York, NY 10016 212-683-8960 Fax 212-213-1539
postmaster@dramatists.com www.dramatists.com

NEW PLAYS

★ **SHEL'S SHORTS by Shel Silverstein.** Lauded poet, songwriter and author of children's books, the incomparable Shel Silverstein's short plays are deeply infused with the same wicked sense of humor that made him famous. "…[a] childlike honesty and twisted sense of humor." *–Boston Herald.* "…terse dialogue and an absurdity laced with a tang of dread give [*Shel's Shorts*] more than a trace of Samuel Beckett's comic existentialism." *–Boston Phoenix.* [flexible casting] ISBN: 0-8222-1897-6

★ **AN ADULT EVENING OF SHEL SILVERSTEIN by Shel Silverstein.** Welcome to the darkly comic world of Shel Silverstein, a world where nothing is as it seems and where the most innocent conversation can turn menacing in an instant. These ten imaginative plays vary widely in content, but the style is unmistakable. "…[*An Adult Evening*] shows off Silverstein's virtuosic gift for wordplay…[and] sends the audience out…with a clear appreciation of human nature as perverse and laughable." *–NY Times.* [flexible casting] ISBN: 0-8222-1873-9

★ **WHERE'S MY MONEY? by John Patrick Shanley.** A caustic and sardonic vivisection of the institution of marriage, laced with the author's inimitable razor-sharp wit. "…Shanley's gift for acid-laced one-liners and emotionally tumescent exchanges is certainly potent…" *–Variety.* "…lively, smart, occasionally scary and rich in reverse wisdom." *–NY Times.* [3M, 3W] ISBN: 0-8222-1865-8

★ **A FEW STOUT INDIVIDUALS by John Guare.** A wonderfully screwy comedy-drama that figures Ulysses S. Grant in the throes of writing his memoirs, surrounded by a cast of fantastical characters, including the Emperor and Empress of Japan, the opera star Adelina Patti and Mark Twain. "Guare's smarts, passion and creativity skyrocket to awesome heights…" *–Star Ledger.* "…precisely the kind of good new play that you might call an everyday miracle…every minute of it is fresh and newly alive…" *–Village Voice.* [10M, 3W] ISBN: 0-8222-1907-7

★ **BREATH, BOOM by Kia Corthron.** A look at fourteen years in the life of Prix, a Bronx native, from her ruthless girl-gang leadership at sixteen through her coming to maturity at thirty. "…vivid world, believable and eye-opening, a place worthy of a dramatic visit, where no one would want to live but many have to." *–NY Times.* "…rich with humor, terse vernacular strength and gritty detail…" *–Variety.* [1M, 9W] ISBN: 0-8222-1849-6

★ **THE LATE HENRY MOSS by Sam Shepard.** Two antagonistic brothers, Ray and Earl, are brought together after their father, Henry Moss, is found dead in his seedy New Mexico home in this classic Shepard tale. "…His singular gift has been for building mysteries out of the ordinary ingredients of American family life…" *–NY Times.* "…rich moments …Shepard finds gold." *–LA Times.* [7M, 1W] ISBN: 0-8222-1858-5

★ **THE CARPETBAGGER'S CHILDREN by Horton Foote.** One family's history spanning from the Civil War to WWII is recounted by three sisters in evocative, intertwining monologues. "…bittersweet music—[a] rhapsody of ambivalence…in its modest, garrulous way…theatrically daring." *–The New Yorker.* [3W] ISBN: 0-8222-1843-7

★ **THE NINA VARIATIONS by Steven Dietz.** In this funny, fierce and heartbreaking homage to *The Seagull*, Dietz puts Chekhov's star-crossed lovers in a room and doesn't let them out. "A perfect little jewel of a play…" *–Shepherdstown Chronicle.* "…a delightful revelation of a writer at play; and also an odd, haunting, moving theater piece of lingering beauty." *–Eastside Journal (Seattle).* [1M, 1W (flexible casting)] ISBN: 0-8222-1891-7

DRAMATISTS PLAY SERVICE, INC.
440 Park Avenue South, New York, NY 10016 212-683-8960 Fax 212-213-1539
postmaster@dramatists.com www.dramatists.com